CLINICAL HANDBOOK OF ADULT EXPLOITATION AND ABUSE

CLINICAL HANDBOOK OF ADULT EXPLOITATION AND ABUSE

Thomas W. Miller, Ph.D., A.B.P.P.
Lane J. Veltkamp, M.S.W., B.C.D.

with contributions by

Lenore E. Walker, Ed.D.
Gary W. Kearl, M.D., M.S.P.H.
Allan L. Beane, Ph.D.
Judith Sheiman, Ph.D., J.D.

INTERNATIONAL UNIVERSITIES PRESS, INC.
MADISON, CONNECTICUT

Library of Congress Cataloging-in-Publication Data

Miller, Thomas W., 1943-
Clinical handbook of adult exploitation and abuse / Thomas W. Miller, Lane J. Veltkamp ; with contributions by Lenore Walker . . . [et al.].
p. cm.
Includes bibliographical references and index.
ISBN 0-8236-0953-7
1. Abused women. 2. Abused men. 3. Psychological abuse. 4. Conjugal violence. 5. Aged—Abuse of. I. Veltkamp, Lane J., 1940- . II. Walker, Lenore E. III. Title.
RC451.4.V53M55 1997
616.85′82—dc21 97-27650
CIP

Manufactured in the United States of America

THIS BOOK IS DEDICATED TO OUR WIVES
JEAN AND MARYBETH
WHOM WE LOVE VERY MUCH

Table of Contents

Preface

This *Clinical Handbook of Adult Exploitation and Abuse* is intended for professionals in the field of health, mental health, child/adult protective services, and law enforcement, who are dealing with abused and neglected adults. We trust that this volume will provide conceptual clarity and scholarly direction in a growing understanding of the most complex and devastating aspects of trauma. It is our intention to build on the important work of several scholars and clinicians who have already contributed to this field of study.

Contained herein is an organized compendium of empirically based observations that should assist the clinician and practitioner in reaching a clearer understanding of victims of adult abuse, making a diagnosis, and developing a treatment plan and intervention strategy that is in the best interests of the individual. In an effort to explicate the nature and consequences of trauma involved in adult abuse, the following are specific objectives to be addressed in this clinical handbook.

1. We want to clearly define adult abuse and provide a framework for understanding its impact on the lives of victims throughout the lifespan.

2. We want to educate professionals regarding the scope of adult abuse, along with its characteristics and efforts.
3. It is our aim to develop a framework by which one can easily understand and recognize the behavioral, psychological, and medical indicators of adult abuse.
4. We have attempted to identify clearly the principles helpful in aiding the legal profession in addressing this complex issue and in providing an appropriate framework from which clinicians can be educated with respect to the legal implications involved in adult abuse.

The impact of abuse knows no geographical boundaries. We trust the readers of this clinical handbook will find the information beneficial in getting a better understanding of the issues and implications in addressing this most important issue.

Lane J. Veltkamp, M.S.W.
Thomas W. Miller, Ph.D.

Acknowledgments

Appreciation is extended to several individuals for their significant contributions to our understanding and to the knowledge base of this most important problem. The published contributions of several scholars and clinicians, such as Lenore Walker, Roland Summit, David Finkelhor, Anne Burgess, Nicholas Groth, Susan Sgroi, and B. Gomez-Schwartz are hereby recognized. Appreciation is also extended to Aline Ludwig, Betty Downing, Tag Heister, Arnold Ludwig, Cathy Smith, Celena Cooper, Janeen Klaproth, Shannon Nelson, Linda Brown, Heather Hosford, Virginia Lynn Morehouse, Janet Saier, and Betty Lawson for their assistance in the preparation of this manuscript.

Acknowledgments

1

Adult Victims of Abuse

Adult abuse, its presence, etiology, and scope, may be for both the victim and the perpetrator, the consequences of childhood maltreatment and abuse. Dating violence among undergraduate students occurs at a rate of 12 to 36 percent, in spite of the fact that not every student surveyed was involved in a dating relationship. Clinical and research data addressing this most serious concern suggest that a violent experience in the family occurs as frequently as every 30 seconds, with close to 50 percent of marriages experiencing some sort of violent episode. Clinicians and researchers who have examined multigenerational family violence recognize that the survivors often suffer from a multiplicity of symptoms, including complicated chronic depression, dissociative disorders, impulsivity, self-mutilation, suicidal ideation and intent, and substance abuse. The resulting symptoms of domestic violence can generate characterological changes seen through personality disorders, difficulty in social and interpersonal relationships throughout the lifespan, somatic disorders, and affective disturbances often seen in prolonged trauma.

Examined herein is the scope of the problem related to adult abuse, as well as characteristics of both perpetrators and victims. The presence of both anxiety and depression in the violent family is often seen in symptoms that include an emerging spectrum disorder, rather than a single psychiatric disorder. Figure 1.1 suggests the various components of this spectrum disorder that often appear in the abusive family. The results of national epidemiological studies have provided convincing evidence that family violence occurs at a higher rate than once suspected. Most clinicians and researchers who study this area believe that dating violence, spouse abuse, and abuse of the elderly tends to be underreported. Abusive situations are often underidentified by health care and mental health practitioners, as well as the court system and the school. This chapter examines important ingredients in understanding the adult abuse.

Ney (1988, see Figure 1.2) describes a triangular model which requires the participation of a perpetrator, a victim, and an observer involved in abusive situations. For example, in spouse abuse the observer is often the child. Discussed are the interactions between persons who assume key roles in abusive relationships. These three core ingredients are not uncommon in the abusive relationships. The observer is important to the perpetrator and the victim because the observer holds a potential solution to the personal dilemmas of both perpetrator and victim. It is not unlikely that the perpetrator and victim will invite or attract an observer to each potential violent event and give that person some authority and some power. The observer can accept that role only on condition that he or she remains relatively anonymous. The observer does not want to be implicated as a party to the violence, either by the victim or the perpetrator, because the judicial system might well hold the observer culpable. It is interesting to note that both the perpetrator and the victim will displace culpability onto the observer if he or she does not perform as expected by either of them. Ney (1988) notes that the observer is attracted to the violence because it provides him or her with the opportunity to examine conflicts which are observed and then enacted. It provides stimulation and it heightens the energy level used in dealing with practical problems within the triad.

Within the adult abuse, observing violence disturbs the personal and interpersonal equilibrium, and there may be situations where the perpetrator is also a victim. In multigenerational abuse, where abuse is a learned experience, often the child victim later in life becomes the adult perpetrator. While some individuals who are victims of abuse

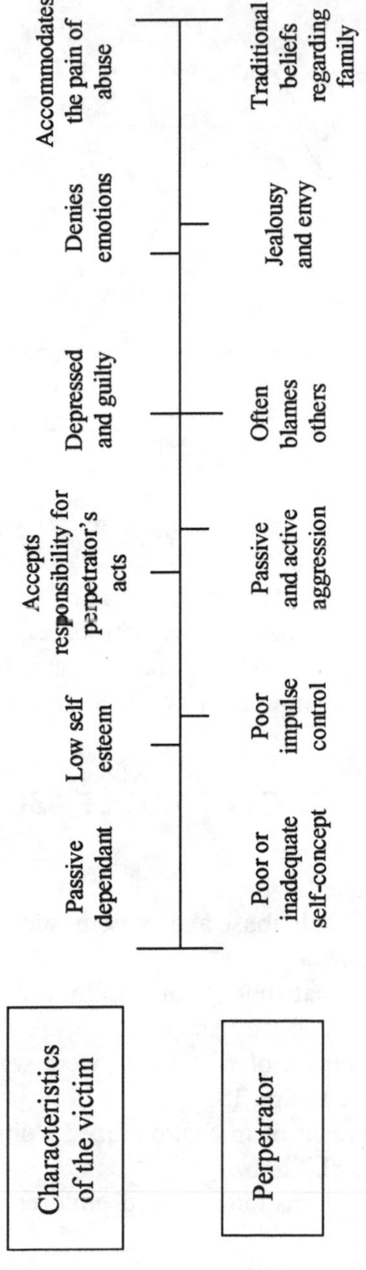

Figure 1.1 Spectrum of Abusive Symptoms for the Victim and Perpetrator

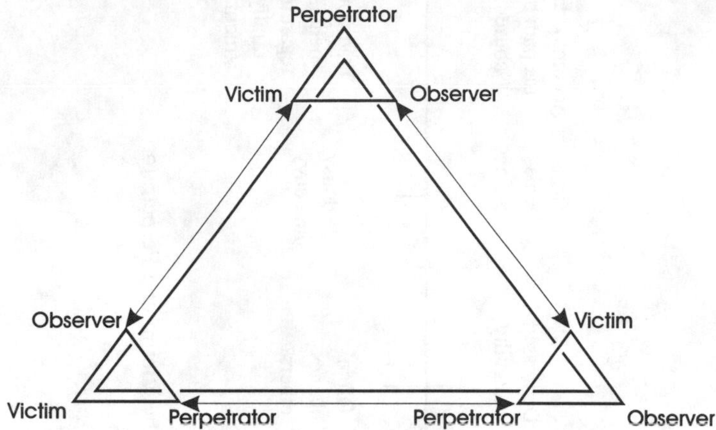

Figure 1.2 Triangles of Abuse (Adapted from Ney [1988])

in childhood integrate their painful experiences and abusive situations and do not continue a cycle of abuse, others perpetuate what they have learned on the next generation. What is most clear is that the impact of an abusive relationship is not easily confined to one generation.

CHARACTERISTICS OF ADULT ABUSE

I. Scope of the problem
  a. Some form of adult abuse and/or domestic violence occurs every 12 seconds.
  b. It is estimated that more than 6 million American adults are abused in some way annually.
  c. Twenty-five percent of all females were sexually misused or abused prior to age 18.
  d. Fifty to 70 percent of institutionalized women were sexually abused as children.
  e. Sixty percent of institutionalized children were sexually abused.

II. Characteristics of the male or female abuser-perpetrator

- **a.** Often comes from a multigenerational pattern of abuse and is aggressive and dependent.
- **b.** Often the victim of "machismo conditioning," which prohibits men from showing pain, sadness, or helplessness, encourages assertive or aggressive behavior.
- **c.** The perpetrator's mother was likely exploited or abused by his or her father.
- **d.** Mother was likely passive and dependent.
- **e.** Perpetrators marry a passive, dependent spouse.
- **f.** Excessive fear of losing spouse.
- **g.** One-third of abusing males also abuse their children.
- **h.** If they abuse their children, one-fourth of the time they abuse their wives.
- **i.** Violence is a way of gaining control in a no support system.
- **j.** Control is a way of gaining self-esteem.
- **k.** The switch to violence is triggered by alcohol 50 percent of the time.
- **l.** The male perpetrator may resent the arrival of children because of his wife's involvement and his own dependency.
- **m.** Inability to handle stress constructively.
- **n.** High level of suspiciousness.

III. Characteristics of adult female victims

- **a.** A multigenerational pattern of abuse may have occurred with the victim having been a victim of child abuse or an observer of spouse abuse as a child.
- **b.** They often do not present as battered; symptoms usually include depression and anxiety and are similar in men.
- **c.** Victim often has left home as an adolescent to escape an abusive situation.
- **d.** Often leaves spouse, only to return later.
- **e.** If the children are abused by the husband, 25 percent of the time the wife is abused.

IV. Characteristics of adult male victims

- **a.** Male victims often have low levels of self-esteem.
- **b.** They tend to be passive-dependent.
- **c.** They comply with and feel responsible for the perpetrator's acts of abuse.

- **d.** They are different from the abused women in the sense that there are few shelters for men; retaliation is often seen as wife abuse, and no one believes the male victim.

V. Children's experiences of adult abuse

- **a.** Often witness abusive acts.
- **b.** The oldest child is often included in the abuse.
- **c.** Symptomatic responses in children who observe abusive situations:
  1. **Preschool child**—symptoms may include hyperactivity, sleep disturbances, eating disturbances, withdrawal, regressions, and delays in development. Inappropriately directed anger, abuse of other children or animals, psychosomatic complaints. **Adolescent**—symptoms often include drug or alcohol abuse, truancy, violence against peers, and suicide gestures.
  2. **Latency age child**—symptoms may include concentration problems, daydreaming, aggressiveness, and withdrawal (see also above No. 1).

VI. Family characteristics

- **a.** Constructive confrontation low, assault high.
- **b.** Support low.
- **c.** Nurturance low.
- **d.** Manipulation high, negotiation low.
- **e.** Family members show symptoms.
- **f.** Difficulty handling feelings constructively.
- **g.** Don't touch each other in constructive ways.
- **h.** High levels of suspiciousness.
- **i.** Don't have a sense of order or responsibility.
- **j.** Lack of productivity.
- **k.** Conflict not resolved.
- **l.** Lack of intimacy and empathy.
- **m.** Mates have similar levels of self-esteem.
- **n.** One parent usually overinvolved with the children.
- **o.** Other parent passive.
- **p.** Marital relationship poor; poor sexual relationship, lack of constructive communication.
- **q.** Generational boundaries unclear.
- **r.** Inappropriate coping skills.

s. Lack of social contacts outside the family.

VII. Diagnostic considerations

a. Abusive male—Intermittent Explosive Disorder (DSM-IV, 312.34) (APA 1994).

b. Abused female—possibly Battered Wife Syndrome (a collection of symptoms including dependency, learned helplessness, accommodation, fear of being alone, violence in family of origin, low self-esteem).

c. Children who observe abuse—possibly PTSD 309.81 or Adjustment Disorder 309.40.

VIII. Areas of clinical exploration with children exposed to adult abuse

a. Peer relationships
b. School-inducing academic performance, behavior, peer relationships
c. Parent–child relationships
d. Drug or alcohol use and/or abuse
e. Fears or inhibitions
f. Aggression, passive behavior
g. Intellectual ability
h. Social skills
i. Role reversal
j. Elevated status and sib group
k. Sleep disturbance
l. Appetite disturbance
m. Child perceived as different
n. Bed-wetting or soiling
o. Regressions
p. Separation problems

IX. Criteria useful in determining degree of psychological harm to the victim.

a. Age of the victim when abuse is occurring
b. Time span involved
c. Degree of aggression
d. Degree of threat
e. The relationship of offender to victim
f. Degree of activity
h. Victim's perception of the abusive events

SPOUSE ABUSE

National studies report that somewhere between 12 and 36 percent of dating couples experience violence in their relationships, even though it has been assumed for years that violence between couples never occurred before the marriage. Research shows that up to 50 percent of married couples experience some form of violence in their relationships. Most commonly, violence assumes the role of pushing or shoving or slapping or hitting, but it can also mean striking with objects, threatening to use objects for abuse, or using weapons or other life-threats.

Jacobson (1995) has developed a typology which attempts to differentiate between the batterers. The type I offender shows the following characteristics: (1) more liberty to be involved outside of marriage; (2) communication style with spouse is circular, going nowhere; (3) the spouse's withdrawal led to an increase in violence; (4) the type I offender was abused as a child in the family of origin; (5) in the two-year study period, there were no divorces or separations in this group, indicating a rather stable, yet violent marital pattern; (6) the women that these men married showed an increase in depression, an increase in fear, and a decrease in the expression of anger; (7) 90 percent of the batterers had personality disorders and drug dependence; (8) anger management programs for this group seem inappropriate.

Treatment Considerations

A. There is a legal obligation to report to appropriate authorities and show empathy toward offender and victim.

B. Inquire about the children, be aware of possible child abuse.

C. Offer support and assistance to victim, including shelter, etc.

D. Instruct the victim on how to find safety and shelter and avoid abusive confrontation—although women do not cause the attack, they sometimes fail to take evasive action to avoid confrontation.

E. Offer a specific program of treatment including group and/or individual therapy for the offender so that he or she may learn impulse control, improve self-esteem, and stop drinking; and then offer group therapy to the victims.

F. Offer group and/or individual therapy for the victims.

Type IIs had the following characteristics: (1) they saw their father being abusive toward their mother; (2) one-third either divorced or separated during the two-year study; (3) they have a wide range of diagnoses; (4) they are less likely to show criminal behavior outside the family.

Women who are victims of abuse in their casual dating relationships are often surprised to find that abuse still occurs and usually escalates once the couple has formalized their relationship through marriage. There is a myth that the abuse will stop and that all of the problems of the relationship will end once the marriage has occurred. Correcting abusive patterns takes work by both persons to learn how to communicate to meet each other's needs more effectively and how to relate fairly within the relationship.

ELDER ABUSE

Intrafamily abuse of the elderly is of growing concern in societies around the world. Elder abuse and neglect are forms of family violence which have been addressed by elder abuse reporting laws from some countries and some U.S. states. Estimates suggest that 500,000 to over a million cases of abuse and neglect of the elderly occur annually in the United States. Accurate detection and assessment of elder abuse victims are critical to understanding the spectrum of family violence.

Definitions of abuse vary widely among the elderly, but generally include such violations of their rights as physical abuse, psychological abuse, active neglect, misuse of drugs, and misuse of property. There are broad parameters for defining elder abuse. Some countries fail to recognize this as a serious problem and, as yet, have not generated reporting laws. Within the concept of intrafamily abuse of the elderly, examined herein are the scope of the problem; characteristics of the abuse itself and of the abused; etiological factors; prevention and treatment factors.

O'Rourke (1981) summarizes seven theories about factors that lead to elder abuse. These include such things as family dynamics,

Table 1.1 Factors Contributing to Elder Abuse and Neglect

Victim–Victimizer Dynamics	*Family Dynamics & Nonsupport*
Disabling illness & caregiver status	Family stress & psychopathology
Dependency and social isolation	Multiple family problems, stress, drugs
Multiple stressors & poor conflict resolution	Changing family roles
Poor anger management skills	Marital conflict related to elderly
Progressive impairments in cognitive functioning	Generational differences
Caregiver stress & abuse history	Life-style dynamics
	Lack of Community Awareness
Societal Insensitivity	Safety and architectural barriers
Public attitude toward needs of the elderly	Ignorance of the legal rights of the elderly
Negative stereotype toward the elderly	Failure of institutions & providers to meet needs
Lack of skill & confidence in social programs	Limited or no follow-up by caregivers
Inadequate resources, poor housing	Bureaucracy at the expense of needed services
Changing societal mores & values	Ignorance of legal needs & rights of elderly
Ignorance of the aging process	

dependence, personality traits, filial crises, internal stress, external stress, and negative attitude toward the elderly. A major premise regarding family dynamics, is that violence is a normative behavioral pattern which is learned in the context of the family. Thus, children learn from observation and participation in the family that violence is an acceptable response to stressful life experiences. Children who have been overdisciplined or abused by parents are more likely to abuse their parents later in life.

Dependence is another important ingredient. The most likely elderly people to be abused are those who are dependent. According to this hypothesis, such impairments as severe physical or mental conditions lead to dependency in the elderly person and this makes him or her vulnerable to abuse. The personality traits hypothesis argues that the offender has personality traits or character disorders that cause him or her to be abusive. Related to this is the fact that adult children are abusive and neglectful because of an abnormal childhood that did not foster their ability to find an appropriate way of dealing with others.

The theory of filial crises argues that elder abuse may be the result of the failure of adult children to resolve a variety of crises between themselves and their parents. Developmental tasks of adult children go beyond the stage of adolescent rebellion, and emancipation from their parents may lead to conflict rather than cooperation in addressing the issues and needs of the elder person. As a result, filial crises occur.

The hypothesis of internal stress argues that the responsibility of providing care and treatment for a dependent elderly person can be so stressful for family members that abusive behavior results.

The external stress hypothesis argues such external factors as economic and financial conditions may result in abusive relationships and therefore contribute to the development of a violent family.

Finally, negative attitudes toward the elderly suggest that patterns of elder abuse as well as neglect, may be reinforced by negative stereotypes toward the elderly and their role and function within our society. Those misconceptions may result in abusive and victimizing situations wherein physical abuse, psychological abuse, financial exploitation, and other violations may be present. What follows are some of the characteristics of elder abuse in the violent family as discussed in *Elder Abuse* (U.S. Department of Health and Human Services, 1980).

CHARACTERISTICS OF ELDER ABUSE

I. Scope of the problem
- **a.** Numerous studies indicate that approximately 10 percent of the aged population in the United States, that is, people aged 65 and older, or 500,000 to one million annually, are abused or neglected.
- **b.** Seventy-five percent of the abuse is physical in nature.
- **c.** Professionals who work with the elderly report 17 percent of the aged population are abused physically, 44 percent are abused verbally.
- **d.** Two-thirds of physical assaults on the elderly are committed by family members.

II. Types of abuse:
- **a.** Physical neglect—The act of omission or failure to provide the necessities, such as medical or dental care, proper diet, or privacy. Thirty-six percent of elderly people report lack

of adequate medical or dental care, approximately 40 percent lack of personal care, and approximately 20 percent report lack of food.

b. Physical abuse—An act of commission carried out with the intention of hurting another person. Thirty-one percent of the elderly report welts or bruises and 15 to 28 percent report direct beatings.

c. Psychological abuse involves infantilization, threats of placing elder in a nursing home, violations of rights, such as withholding medication or health aids (i.e., false teeth, eye glasses, or hearing aids). Within this abused group of elderly, one-third report isolation, another third report verbal assaults, and nearly half report intimidation and threats.

d. Material abuse may involve misuse of money or property, which was reported by 46 percent; and theft of money or property reported by 12 to 18 percent.

e. Sexual abuse—Statistics are not clear regarding the true incidence of sexual abuse of the elderly.

III. Characteristics of the abuser

a. Age: 53 percent are middle aged; 12 percent are teenagers.

b. Sex: 58 percent are female.

c. Economic: 65 percent are middle income, 12 percent are lower income.

d. Relationship to victim: 42 percent are children, 19 percent are grandchildren, 12 percent are spouses (Pollick, 1987).

IV. Characteristics of the abused

a. Sex: 81 percent are female.

b. Race: 88 percent are white; 12 percent nonwhite.

c. Living arrangements: 46 percent live with their children; 31 percent live with their grandchildren.

d. Economic level: 58 percent are middle income; 27 percent are retired on a pension (e.g., social security).

e. Degree of impairment: 62 percent are unable to prepare food; 62 percent need help in keeping clean; 54 percent cannot take their own medication without assistance; 19 percent are bedridden; 19 percent have impaired mobility.

V. Reaction of the abused:

a. Denial (28%)

b. Resignation (20%)
c. Withdrawal (16%), isolation (16%)
d. Fear (12%)
e. Depression (8%)
f. Abuse of drugs (24%)

VI. Etiology

Family dysfunction in childhood leads to disintegrated personal relationships characterized by problem avoidance and failure in self-protection. These problematic relationships lead to adult crises and parental dependency which in turn cause situational conflicts. These conflicts escalate at times of stress or tension and lead to the mistreatment of older family members. This maltreatment is reinforced if victim compliance is attained. Maltreatment is viewed by the abuser as the "solution to the problem."

VII. Prevention

a. Increased resources to caregivers, such as home aides, medical and nursing care, meal delivery, day care programs, educational programs, regarding nutrition and physical care, and counseling programs.

b. Increased resources to the older person, such as recreational programs, leisure opportunities, and help with maintaining independence.

VIII. Treatment

a. If improved social policy is to take place, public policy must be designed to alleviate problems created by family maltreatment of elders. First, there must be acknowledgement of elder abuse as a social problem. Second, there must be development of specific procedures to deal with problems. Third, there must be assignment of resources to develop programs; for example, the creation of an elder abuse preventive and treatment act on a national level would help focus attention on this problem. Mandatory reporting laws help the elderly and other family members focus on stopping abusive behavior.

b. Intervention

1. Shelters and access to available services, including legal services must be arranged.

2. Psychological services need to be family oriented, designed to preserve the family if appropriate, and focus on multigenerational patterns of abuse.
3. Steps:
   a. Victim protection—both medical and psychological aspects are equally important.
   b. Awareness of assault on other family members, specifically spouse and children.
   c. Focus on offender by making treatment mandatory.
   d. Focus on marital relationship.
   e. Focus on the abusing member's relationship with persons outside the family system; increase the support system.
   f. Provide counseling as appropriate for victim and perpetrator(s).

CONCLUDING THOUGHTS

Recognizing the cycle of violence (Walker, 1994) is essential in understanding and addressing family violence. Families at risk for violence appear to have two elements in their history: a multigenerational pattern of abuse and a particular family constellation.

The multigenerational pattern of abuse is perpetuated by individuals who witness and learn violence as a model of behavior and pass this model on to succeeding generations, thereby continuing the cycle of violence. Examples of this include physical, psychological, and sexual rituals passed on from one generation to the next such as punitive methods of discipline. Similarly blood-pinnings in the military serve to perpetuate punitive rituals which exemplify the cycle of violence. Clinical research has shown that persons most prone to violent behavior may share certain common experiences, including witnessing parental violence during childhood, low self-esteem, difficulty controlling anger, impulsive behavior, isolation from others, and minimal family and social support.

In identifying adults at risk, it is important to recognize the following indicators:

- A person who may be extremely passive and dependent or reluctant to assert her or himself for fear of destroying the family unit.
- A perpetrator who turns to the spouse or child to relieve or displace anger, frustration, or hostility.
- A poor marital relationship that shows minimal constructive communication and poor interpersonal relations.
- Relationships characterized by enmeshment.
- Minimal social contacts outside the family.
- Adults who have poor skills in coping with anxiety and stress within the family situation.
- The family as a whole has poor communication skills.
- Families develop a barrier that prevents external intervention in the cycle of violence.

Summarized in Table 1.2 are physical and behavioral indicators of adult abuse most often seen in their victims. The core ingredients of physical or psychological abuse are a difficult experience for anyone to understand and accommodate. ''Trauma Accommodation Syndrome'' (Miller and Veltkamp, 1989a) attempts to outline how trauma, such as abuse, is processed by the victim. This model is important because the victim usually has extreme difficulty in discussing any aspect of the victimization. A victim of severe abuse often passes through a series of stages in dealing with the trauma. The initial and most traumatic stage is the process of victimization; this is the stressor resulting in acute physical or psychological traumatization. This traumatization can take many forms and is not defined merely by physical abuse. Modern research no longer views abuse as being an ''anger'' or ''control'' problem on the part of the abuser. Instead, the perpetrator's acts of abuse and intimidation are seen as deliberate and intentional acts focused on dominating and controlling the abused in all areas of his or her life. The Duluth Abuse Intervention Project (1992) is considered by many professionals working in the area of domestic violence to be one of the most comprehensive programs to address domestic violence. It has identified critical factors important in recognition and resolution of domestic conflicts and how perpetrators confuse and control their partners' issues of power and control. The behaviors used by batterers between abusive incidents to scare, manipulate, silence, confuse, and control their partners are depicted.

Table 1.2 Symptoms of Abuse and Neglect

Physical Indicators	Behavioral Indicators
Family Violence	
Unexplained bruises and welts	Emotional constriction and blunted affect
Unexplained burns, especially on soles, palms, back, or buttocks	Extreme withdrawal or aggressiveness
Immersion burns	Extreme rejection or dependence on caregivers
Rope burns on arms, legs, neck, or torso	Apprehension, fearfulness
Unexplained fractures, e.g., to skull, nose, or facial structure; in various stages of healing; multiple or spiral fractures of arms or legs	Fear of going
	Depression
	Phobias, anxiety
	Sleep disturbance
Unexplained lacerations or abrasions to mouth, lips, gums, eyes, or external genitalia	Withdrawn, inhibited behavior
	Obsessive–compulsive behavior
Sexual Abuse	
Difficulty in walking or sitting	Sleep disturbances
Torn, stained, or bloody underclothing	Withdrawn or regressed behavior
Bruises or bleeding in external genitalia, vaginal, or anal areas	Secondary enuresis or encopresis
	Bizarre, sophisticated, or unusual sexual behavior or knowledge
	Poor interpersonal skills
	Self-report of abuse
	Anorexia
	Extreme self-blame
	Extreme fears
Neglect	
	Begging, stealing food, homeless
	Fatigue, listlessness, depression
	Delinquency (e.g., thefts, vandalism)
	Victim reports that there is no caregiver

The battering incidents themselves, according to Walker (1996) should be referred to as "torture." These "incidents" may include physical, mental, or sexual abuse and/or scare tactics. A review of some of the techniques used to gain domination and control by abusers is summarized in Table 1.3.

Table 1.3 Factors of Power and Control in Abusive Relationships

Intimidation	*Emotional Abuse*
Smashing things Destroying property Abusing pets Displaying weapons Creating fear and apprehension	Putting victim down Making victim feel bad Calling names Playing mind games Humiliating victim Making victim feel guilty
Coercion and Threats	*Isolation*
Threatening to leave to commit suicide Threatening to hurt others Threatening to kill others	Controlling access to whom victim sees and talks with Limiting outside involvement Using jealousy to justify actions
Economic Abuse	*Minimizing, Denying, and Blaming*
Preventing victim from keeping a job Making victim ask for money Giving an allowance Taking victim's money	Making light of the abuse Saying the abuse didn't happen Shifting responsibility for abusive behavior

People's response to abuse, intimidation, or attempts to dominate is to feel overwhelmed and to feel totally out of control; they are controlled externally. After the trauma, it is not uncommon for the victim to think repeatedly of the event, focusing on the intimidating act, as well as the physical pain of the abuse.

This acute stage of trauma is followed by cognitive disorganization and confusion marked by a vagueness in understanding both why the abuse occurred and the expectations and demands of the perpetrator. The third stage frequently involves denial and a conscious inhibition of thoughts and feelings to minimize the trauma. This conscious inhibition may involve the person relapsing into the cognitive disorganization phase with flashbacks to the acute physical and psychological trauma. Often in this stage the victim exhibits classic avoidant behavior and is not aware of his or her effort to avoid the psychological trauma associated with the abuse. In this stage, the victim unconsciously denies the abuse and will not respond to the experience of abuse. This third stage results in stagnation, feelings of entrapment, denial of the extent

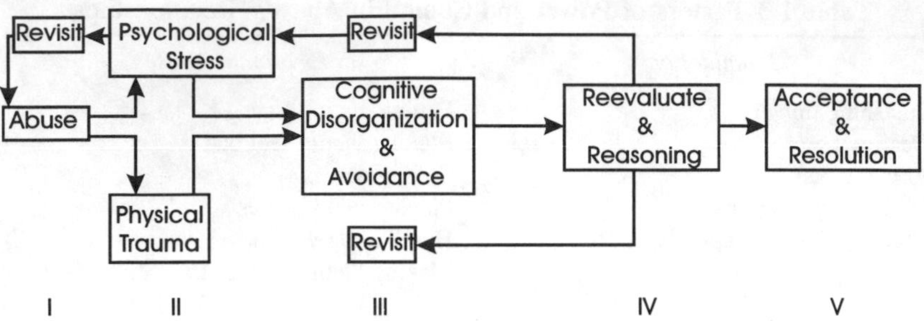

Figure 1.3 Processing Adult Abuse

of the abuse, and can result in the victim accommodating herself to the pain of the abuse.

This avoidant stage may be followed by a stage of therapeutic reevaluation, wherein a significant other supports the individual in reasoning through and reevaluating the psychological and physical trauma associated with the abuse. In this stage, the victim may begin to disclose specific incidents of abuse. This phase of therapeutic reevaluation and reasoning is significant because it indicates that conscious support has been realized by the victim in passing from the avoidant phase to the issues, activities, and trauma of the abusing experience(s).

The final stage is one of coping or resolution, wherein the victim has dealt with the issues and come to a better understanding of the significance of the abuse and the perpetrator. The victim is viewed at this stage as: (1) being more open to talking about the incident; (2) being able to express thoughts and feelings more readily; and (3) being engaged in both assessment and therapy to discharge some of the aggressive feelings toward the perpetrator. At this final stage, the individual has developed an alliance with significant others or professionals and is able to: (1) explore the original traumatic experience; (2) deal with both the physical and psychological stressors involved; (3) attend to repressed material and the process of either conscious inhibition or unconscious denial utilized during the avoidant stage; (4) focus on self-understanding and receive psychological and emotional support from others in attempting to comprehend the rationale for the abusing experiences; (5) explore appropriate psychosocial life-styles to determine the degree of therapeutic intervention yet required.

Treatment of the victim and the offender is a complex process which may involve several professionals. Collaboration, cooperation, mutual respect, and understanding of each other's roles are essential to the success of the treatment process (Miller and Veltkamp, 1989a). Reporting laws have been adopted in most states recognizing the need for open communication in the area of abuse. These laws recognize no privileged relationships beyond that of attorney and client. In abuse of a spouse or of the elderly, perpetrators may have been abused or exposed to similar violent themes and experience symptoms. Children may feel guilt that they did not try to intervene and stop the abuse. The following are important areas for consideration when working with victims.

1. Determine if victims have been abused.
2. Preserve the psychological bond with their caregivers.
3. Preserve continuity of relationships and place.
4. Reduce risk for victims by providing supervision (i.e., monitor the relationship with the perpetrator).
5. Evaluate to determine if victims are showing symptoms.
6. If victims cannot be protected in their home, they should be removed.

The offender must be the focus of prevention and treatment. Historically, communities have upheld the offender's continuance of the abusive patterns by asking the wrong questions about the abuse. The most frequently asked question has been, Why doesn't she leave? What did she do to cause the abuse? Increasingly, communities, social service agencies, prosecutors, and researchers are asking very different questions such as, What will stop the abuse? Should the offender go to jail? How do we protect the women and children? How do we stop the abuse from continuing? Is the family treatable? Can they be rehabilitated or reunited?

Programs for intervening with families to stop the cycle of abuse require coordinated efforts between law enforcement, the courts, and social agencies. The most successful programs require that the offender understand that there are consequences for their actions including arrest and incarceration. The focus of abuser treatment programs is to assist them in breaking through denial and taking responsibility for their actions. They must also be helped to examine and change sexist beliefs that elevate men to positions of power within their households. They must be taught to analyze and understand their cultural conditioning which views violence as an acceptable method of dominating their victims, and to learn healthy and nonviolent ways to respond to conflict (Paymer, 1996).

The impact and long-term effects of adult abuse need further research, including the various forms of abuses from emotional abuse to physical battering. Ways to encourage reporting, so that the number of unreported cases is reduced, need the immediate attention and sensitivity of health care professionals. Clearly, adult abuse is not limited to any particular socioeconomic level or specific population of individuals, but has been found to be more prevalent among families experiencing financial pressures, frequent moves, alcohol and drug use, high stress, isolation from peer groups and family support systems, and a history of domestic violence.

Strong and consistent community response must include a multidisciplinary approach. There must be an educational approach that mandates reports of all domestic violence. The police must respond in a firm manner, arresting violent offenders and using incarceration, which communicates a clear message that violence will not be tolerated. Judges must be educated in the use of incarceration, emergency protective orders, and treatment. Health care providers must be trained to handle emergencies appropriately, believe and support the victim and report the abuse. And finally, mental health providers must be trained in specialized treatment strategies for adolescent and adult victims, juvenile and adult offenders, as well as specialized treatment strategies with a community response designed to solve this devastating problem.

2

Clinical Theories of Adult Abuse

The spectrum of adult abuse ranges from dating relationships, spouse and partner abuse, to elder abuse. Within this construct and the spectrum of persons across the life span, there are a variety of mediums of abuse as well. From physical abuse to passive neglect, from active neglect to psychological abuse, financial abuse, sexual abuse, all involving violations of trust and a lack of the respect one human being should have for another's dignity. In examining the clinical theories of adult abuse, we shall explore the key components of the adult victim and perpetrator and attempt to improve our understanding of the precipitating and contributing factors, as well as the emotional consequences involved in the processing of abuse from the perspective of both victim and perpetrator.

Couched within the theoretical basis of adult abuse are a series of critical factors that include intrapersonal dynamics, stress dependency, and intergenerational transmission of violent behavior. Theoretical models that address traumatization and learned helplessness, bonding and attachment theory, and object relations theory are among the most compelling in aiding our understanding of the clinical theories of adult abuse. In addition to these are models of situational stress, additive burden, and chronic burden that contribute to our understanding of domestic violence. Examined herein are the spectrum of abusive relationships and the victim–victimizer relationship and its interface with current theoretical positions.

THEORETICAL BASES OF ADULT ABUSE

The evolution of the understanding of abuse trauma consists of examining the physical, emotional, and sexual abuse of the victim. Briere (1992) has suggested that the earliest attention emanated from medical professionals who focused primarily on the diagnosis of physical abuse. It was mental health professionals who seemed to show an increased interest in this area and concentrated on the incidence not only of physical abuse but sexual abuse too. Briere and others have suggested that those concerned about physical abuse have maintained that the field of abuse study has developed into an examination of the prevalent forms of abuse and the potential psychological impact on the victim. They have also argued that this focus has created a competitive marketplace which may not, at this point, be in the best interest of the victim.

Hart and Brassard (1987) suggest that emotional abuse is inherent in all forms along the abuse spectrum, and that the major negative impact of all abuse is psychologically based. Van der Kolk (1987), Herman (1992), and Briere (1992), as well as McCann and Pearlman (1990) in their discussion, suggested that the same risk factors that face adults in traumatization may also face the child who is victimized and traumatized. Miller and Veltkamp (1988) introduced the trauma accommodation syndrome and adapted this model to the impact and processing of traumatization in both children and adults who may be victims of abuse.

Steele (1986) suggests that we continue to be concerned about the long-term impact of child abuse and resulting impact on adults. Veltkamp, Miller, and Silman (1994) discusses the issues of adult non-survivors of child abuse (victims who adapt poorly to their traumatization) and present concepts of how these individuals attempt to cope.

Herman (1992) illustrates the intensity of child abuse by emphasizing that many traumatic events, such as rape or battery are single, circumscribed incidents, while child abuse tends to be a repeated trauma and as such, has a propensity to become chronic and with greater psychological damage than perhaps other forms of traumatizing experiences. An earlier study by Herman (1981) suggests that 38 percent of adult women reported incestuous or extrafamilial sexual abuse during childhood. Prevalence rates such as this reflect difficulties in adjustment in adult life and add to the growing literature aimed at documenting the long-term effects of child sexual abuse.

Of significant importance to the victim is that unlike adults who suffer traumatization, children who are traumatized through abuse endure such experiences during critical developmental stages in their life. Briere (1984) has generated a typology of parent or caretaker behaviors. These include:

- A rejecting caregiver
- Degrading or devaluating the victim
- Terrorizing the victim
- Isolating the victim
- Corrupting/missocializing the victim
- Exploitation
- Deprivation of love, sensitivity, and emotional response
- Contradictory, ambivalent, unreliable, and inconsistent caregiving.

McCann, Sakheim, and Abrahamson (1988) reviewed the empirical literature on psychological responses to victimization and identified a variety of responses that may be recognized by the victim. The spectrum of responses varies from emotional to cognitive, behavioral, interpersonal, and biological. Emotional response patterns tend to relate to traumatic victimization and include fear and anxiety, depression, decreased self-esteem, uncertainty about identity, guilt, shame, and anger. Cognitive disturbances seem to be related to perceptual problems and dissociation. Perceptual disturbances are typically labeled posttraumatic stress, and central to this category is the reexperiencing of the trauma through flashbacks or nightmares related to the trauma. Briere offered an expanded description of posttraumatic stress and indicated that central to the symptoms of traumatization and stress are sudden sensory memories, such as visual images of the perpetrator or hearing the perpetrator during flashbacks and nightmares.

Traumatic victimization with dissociative features has been defined by McCann and Pearlman (1990) as a defensive disruption in the normally occurring connections between feelings, thoughts, behaviors, and memories. The dissociative component is related to psychologically traumatic events and is seen as a coping mechanism that offers escape from reality (Van der Kolk and Kadish, 1987; Putnam, 1989). It also permits traumatic memories to be harnessed outside the realm of conscious awareness and creates a detachment from self so that the trauma seems to be happening in someone else or in a depersonalized self. It is, in its truest self, an emotional analgesic that separates the victim's pain from the victimization itself.

Biological components of traumatization include a broader spectrum of accommodating traumatization and stress. Clark and Miller (1996, see Figure 2.1) describe this traumatization process within the concept of the biochemical markers noted in the accommodation of trauma process.

The psychological responses to victimization are commonly seen in behavioral response patterns. Briere (1992) suggests that alcohol and substance abuse are means by which the individual attempts to cope with the impact of traumatization resulting from being victimized. It is, in many ways, a self-prescribed method of dealing with the anxiety, depression, and traumatic events and memories one realizes in the victimization process.

The behavioral response pattern can be seen in the process of self-mutilization, a debilitating, non-life-threatening measure used to deal with victimization. Similarly, eating disorders are not necessarily a result of abuse but have been documented as the long-term behavioral effects of dealing with the distress of victimization and long-term adaptation to abuse.

THE AFFILIATION HYPOTHESIS

The affiliation hypothesis addressed in understanding the traumatization process has been discussed by Herman (1992). It argues that children's emotional development is closely affiliated with the basic issues

Figure 2.1 Biological consequences of stress and trauma

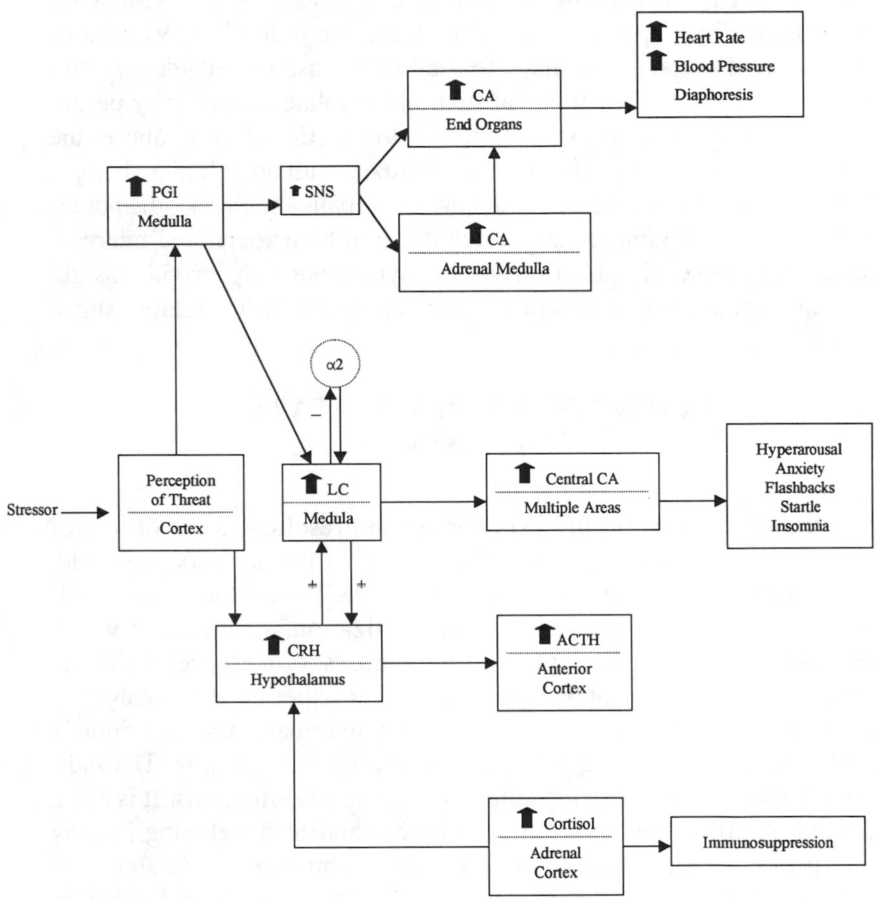

PGI:	nucleus paraglgantocellutaris
LC:	locus coeruleus
SNS:	sympathetic nervous system
α2:	alpha-2 adrenergic receptors
—:	negative feedback inhibition
+:	positive feedback stimulation
CA:	catecholamine
CRH:	corticotropin-releasing hormone
ACTH:	adrenocorticotropin hormone

From: D. Clarke & T. W. Miller (1996), Clinical models of traumatization in children. Pittsburgh, PA: University of Pittsburgh, Typescript.

of trust, autonomy, safety, and security, and is closely associated to the first caregiver's relationship with the victim. It is this first experience that forms the basis for future relationships and provides the sense of individuality, separateness, and trust for the individual. Victims of childhood abuse suffer damage to the basic sense of self-identity and lose a sense of trust when this affiliation is violated, usually by perpetrators who are known to the child. To the victim of child abuse, the human connection, the affiliation one realizes with other human beings, may well become associated with emotional pain and impact the potential intimacy a person realizes in adult life in both social and interpersonal experiences. Implications of this hypothesis may provide insight into important components in the development of adult relationships.

TRAUMATIZATION AND LEARNED HELPLESSNESS

The impact of stressful life experiences and resulting sense of loss of control or helplessness is indeed a pervasive theme associated with traumatization spectrum. Van der Kolk (1987) and others have indicated that the effects of repeated traumatization, such as that which occurs in abused children, partners, or spouses, often leaves a chronic sense of helplessness or victimization. This experience is thought to be so psychologically overwhelming that it impairs the individual's ability to develop coping behaviors or coping mechanisms. The individual loses a sense of being able to influence life situations. It is often related to difficulties in relating to others and to developing healthy interpersonal relationships. Victims of child abuse or spouse abuse are said to suffer from this loss of trust and confidence in others. Veltkamp, Miller, and Silman (1994) discuss the vulnerability experienced in adult relationships that result from traumatization experienced as a child. Herman (1992) has suggested that adult survivors of child abuse harbor deep-rooted desires to relive earlier traumatic experiences and make these events demonstrate a different, varied, and perhaps more positive outcome. Similarly, Miller and Veltkamp (1989b), in the trauma accommodation syndrome, argue that adult survivors move through a series of stages or phases that argue in favor of a revisiting and reprocessing of the traumatization experienced as a child.

COGNITIVE PROCESSING AND TRAUMATIZATION

Stressful life events are often unpredictable. Horowitz (1986) suggests a model of normal stress response. It is argued in this model that during and immediately following the trauma of adult abuse, the victim often attempts to organize, process, and integrate an overwhelming amount of stimulation. This results in information overload and may cause people to experience a state of stress until they are able to process all of the information. Often, the mind alternates between two levels of functioning: (1) compulsive repetition of memories about the trauma, or (2) denial or withdrawal from such traumatic thoughts. Horowitz argues that compulsion repetitions can include intrusive thoughts, such as flashbacks and nightmares, as well as emotional reactions, such as flashbacks of feelings that were experienced during the original traumatic event. Horowitz also argues that repression or denial of the events may occur, wherein the individual attempts to detach him or herself from the cognitions or emotions of the traumatizing experience.

FEAR NETWORK AND TRAUMATIZATION

Foa, Riggs, Dancer, and Rothbaum (1993), suggest that traumatization processing involves the formation of a fear network which includes three kinds of information: "Information about the feared stimulus, information about verbal, physiological, and overt behavioral responses, and interpretive information about the meaning of the stimulus and response events of the stressful life event" (p. 27). Fear reduction requires two conditions. First, the fear structure must be activated by fear relevant information. Second, in order to modify the memory network which is incompatible with information in the fear structure that must be made available, an effective processing of the incompatible information may well lead to dissociation of response elements from the stimulus elements in the fear structure. Furthermore, this may result in a modification of information about the meaning of the feared stimuli and responses. And, finally, normal coping with traumatic events may include the successful application of both conditions, as stated.

COGNITIVE PROCESSING MODEL AND TRAUMATIZATION

A cognitive processing model, based on postulations of Horowitz (1986), suggests the processing of variables that mediate the influence of the traumatic event. These variables are divided into a series of stages which include network formation, wherein a network of trauma related to the memories is formed. The formation of this network is determined by the characteristics of the traumatic experience, which includes stimulus, response, and meaning to the victim.

Pretrauma personality and past experiences are important components to understanding how adaptation occurs in this model. Creamer argues that victims who engage in the network resolution processing and use avoidance moderately tend to recover from the traumatizing event, while others are at risk to develop traumatic stress disorder symptoms which are more likely to result in excessive avoidance and inability to modify the memory network.

ATTACHMENT THEORY AND TRAUMATIZATION

At the core of attachment theory and traumatization is the work of Bowlby (1969), who focused on the biologically driven emotional attachment between parent and child. This process may have implications for understanding the adult abusive relationship. Bowlby argues that the human need for deep emotional attachment is tied to evolutionary development, genetics, and the biologically driven focus that drives offspring to attach themselves to caregivers in order to maintain a constant contact with a protecting figure. The protector provides the safety signal and the realization that the offspring can explore the surrounding world without fear of harm. Abusive situations challenge the safety signal and provide emotional conflict that requires the child to maneuver psychologically and attempt to reestablish a sense of safety. Where this process is not easily accomplished, anxiety and depression may follow. Issues of trust and autonomy occur and a neurobiological sensitivity to abandonment is triggered. The ultimate impact of this relates to identity and intimacy issues in adult life and may result in difficulties with or fear of intimacy and attachment in the victim.

TRAUMATIC BONDING THEORY

Dutton and Painter (1981) have suggested a theory of ''traumatic bonding'' wherein powerful emotional attachments are seen to develop from two specific features of abusive relationships: (1) power imbalances, and (2) intermittent good and bad treatment. This notion, that attachment is strengthened by intermittent abuse, appears, at first glance, to be somewhat at odds with the classic attachment theory, which proposes that attachment increases with consistent positive treatment.

Dutton and Painter (1981) point out a method that helps to understand a pathway into an abusive relationship and how it constitutes a form of social entrapment. The initial abusive incident often appears to be an anomaly which occurs at a time when the relationship is new and feelings of both parties are positive. This, coupled with a lack of severity, operates to strengthen the effective attachment at a time when the belief has not yet formed that the abuse would be repetitive and possibly inescapable.

Dutton and Painter suggest that repeated incidents of greater severity tend to shift the cognitions to the belief that the violence will recur unless the victim does something to prevent it. Dutton and Painter further discuss the reasons for this initial introjection of blame for the abuse. There are two structural features in the apparently diverse relationships where traumatic bonding has been described. The first feature is the existence of a power imbalance, wherein the maltreated person perceives him or herself to be subjugated or dominated by the other. The second is the intermittent nature of the abuse, wherein the authors argue that intermittency and power imbalances are quintessential features of abusive relationships. Research studies addressing traumatic bonding have tended to conclude that economic, rather that psychological variables, were better predictors of victims who tend to stay in abusive relationships. Financial factors involve a variety of issues that contribute to the victim's economic dependence on the perpetrator.

CYCLE OF VIOLENCE THEORY

Lenore Walker (1992, see Figure 2.2) has generated a cyclical pattern of domestic violence that approximates the intermittent punishment–indulgence pattern, not unlike some aspects of "traumatic bonding." In the cyclical pattern of domestic violence outlined by Walker, tension gradually builds during an initial phase, a battering incident occurs in a second phase, and a calming respite follows in the third phase.

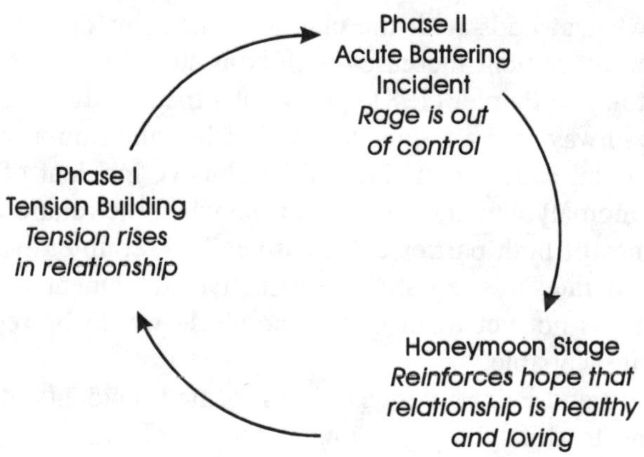

Figure 2.2 Lenore Walker's Cycle Theory of Violence

Best known as the "battered woman syndrome," the victim's psychological reactions in each of the three phases, and the repetition of these phase-related responses, serve to bond the battered woman to her batterer just as strongly as "miracle" glue binds inanimate substances. The result of the battering incident and the cycle of violence, usually involves guilt and contrition, leads to an attempt to make amends, and the belief that the relationship can survive, which becomes a part of the victim's perception of the relationship. This finding is consistent with the traumatic bonding situation and theory and suggests that abuse occurs intermittently.

The other side of the abusing situation is likely to be characterized by the onset of positive behaviors, as described by Walker (1979), this being the contrition phase in the cycle of violence. The victim is subject to alternating periods of aversive negative arousal and the release associated with the removal of aversive arousal. It is not uncommon for the perpetrator to promise to change, no longer be abusive, and make further commitments to a loving relationship. The model of alternating aversive and pleasant conditions is, in fact, an experimental paradigm within learning theory, known as intermittent reinforcement-punishment, which is highly effective in producing consistent patterns of behavior that are difficult to extinguish or terminate and which develop the strongest experimentally produced emotional bonds.

OBJECT RELATIONS THEORY AND TRAUMATIZATION

Object relations theory, which is psychoanalytically oriented, argues that a relationship exists between those who actually function in the external real world and those individuals who have *images* of what might exist in the real world. Implications raised by object relations theory, while primarily useful in understanding child abuse, may also provide insight into circumstances that lead to adult abuse.

Object relations theory evolved into an orientation suggesting that early images the child experiences become enduring representations and ultimately shape the developmental and emerging adult interpersonal life. Krugman (1987) argues that the pivotal nature of object relations theory, as it is applied to traumatization, involves the range of reactions experienced by the victim with both primary and secondary elaborations.

The primary elaboration is argued by Horowitz (1986) wherein a biphasic alteration between intrusion and denial occurs in the victim. The result is that the traumatized person often avoids intimacy or has difficulty engaging in effective interpersonal relations. Unresolved traumatic experiences are thought to impair the object relational world of the traumatized person and have direct applicability to the experience victims often relate when they have experienced physical or sexual abuse. Object relations theory then involves early childhood–caregiver interactions that are thought to affect the person's internally developing images of him or herself, and the relationship to other individuals, which shape the quality of what interpersonal relationships might then be realized in adulthood.

INFORMATION PROCESSING AND TRAUMA

Burgess and Hartman (1993) propose a model of information processing of traumatic events that can include family violence and other forms of adult abuse. This model involves four phases: first is a pretrauma phase that includes the individual and social context variables prior to the traumatic event. Factors, such as socioeconomic status, structure and dynamics of family life, parental attitudes, dependencies, and adaptation skills are important ingredients in the pretrauma phase. Burgess and Hartman argue that there are two processes that occur in this phase: trauma learning and trauma replay.

Trauma learning refers to the outcome to a biphasic alarm response, namely, "the arousal and dissociation processes specific to survival and the protection of physical and psychic integretity," (Burgess and Hartman, 1993, p. 51). This process is marked by chronic tension, arousal, avoidance, numbing, and intrusive thoughts of the trauma. The trauma replay refers to the reenactment, repetition, and displacement of the abusive experience. The next phase, disclosure, can have positive or negative effects, depending on the reaction of the support system, the family, and the community. During the final phase, posttrauma, numerous outcomes may arise ranging from psychiatric disorder to successful adaptation to the trauma.

RAPE TRAUMA SYNDROME

The impact of rape on both the primary and secondary victims is a major aspect of adult abuse. The Rape Trauma Syndrome (Burgess and Holstrom, 1979) summarizes a series of stages or phases that a victim experiences as a result of rape and its subsequent trauma. National crime survey statistics, provided through the U.S. Department of Justice, estimate that as many as 5 percent of women have been victims of attempted rape. There are believed to be an even greater number of unreported secondary victims when a rape occurs such as the significant others of rape victims whose relationships–marriages are affected by the crime, and children who have been witnesses to the rape of a parent.

The rape trauma syndrome was first described by Burgess and Holstrom (1979) involving, initially, a two-stage syndrome of disorganization, which was seen as the acute phase, and a stage of reorganization. An intermediate phase between the two, called outward adjustment, suggested that victims of rape appear outwardly composed, generally denying and repressing feelings. This stage is preceded by the acute phase, which includes shock and anger, disbelief, a desire for revenge, denial, anxiety, guilt, embarrassment, of humiliation. Also, a key component in the acute phase is a feeling of both helplessness and dependence where the victim may seek help or may remain secretive about the rape experience. In the organizational phase, Burgess and Holstrom suggest that the victim may experience such things as sexual dysfunction, phobia, sleep disorder, anxiety, and an urge to talk about and resolve the feelings experienced by the initial crime. During this phase, the victim may work toward an accommodation or resolution to the situation, as suggested by Miller and Veltkamp (1993), in their trauma accommodation syndrome, or remain secretive and retract the initial effort to confront or address the traumatizing experience. The victim of rape usually feels physically and emotionally violated. The loss of control over their personhood and their autonomy may often lead to the development of obsessional thoughts about the rape experience. Depending on where the rape occurred, the person's feelings of safety and security are clearly disrupted. Fears may be generalized to all individuals who resemble the perpetrator. Various versions of the rape trauma syndrome have included an acute phase, outward adjustment, reorganization phase, and resolution, which is summarized in Figure 2.3.

By DSM-IV (APA, 1994a) standards, both the acute and chronic traumatization of rape must be recognized within the context of the

Figure 2.3 Rape Trauma Syndrome

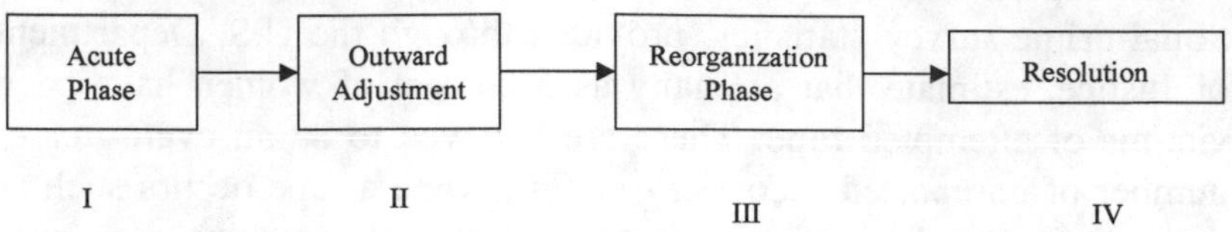

anxiety disorders, including acute traumatic stress disorder and post-traumatic stress disorder. The psychological impact arising from the stressor of rape on the internal self and subsequent feelings, thoughts, fantasies, and impulses often includes dissociation. The dissociation results in regression of adaptive techniques, higher levels of defenses, cognitive dysfunction, poorer reality testing, and secondary processing of the thoughts and feelings related to the rape. Victims are usually left with serious problems in trusting others, as well as themselves, as a result of the rape. Feelings of autonomy and self-assertiveness are often deflated, for the experience of rape is not only an attack on autonomy, but it is, as well, an attack on self-confidence and self-esteem. The issue of the safety signal has been challenged, and the resulting symptoms are quite consistent with the silent reaction to trauma, resulting in avoidant behavior, distancing, depression, and likely use of substances to cope with the experience.

The acute medical consequences of the rape experience fall into four main categories:

1. Nongenital injuries;
2. Genital injuries;
3. Sexually transmitted disease;
4. Pregnancy

Each of these categories must be addressed in the "Acute Phase" noted in Figure 2.3. Emergency medical treatment must be provided to address the key issues related to the rape experience.

Human clinical behavior is a critical ingredient in allowing the individual who has experienced this traumatization to address the essential issues necessary in attempting recovery and readjustment.

Figure 2.4 outlines and identifies key areas necessary in addressing the issues; see also the American Association Medical Council on Scientific Affairs (1994) *Report on Violence against Women: Relevance for Medical Practitioners.*

REMER'S EMPOWERMENT MODEL (1986)

The Empowerment Model is a feminist-oriented approach to therapeutic intervention for rape survivors and consists of six recovery stages: (1) prestage; (2) rape event; (3) crisis and disorganization; (4) outward satisfactory adjustment and denial; (5) reliving and working through; (6) resolution and integration. Remer identifies corresponding counseling strategies for each stage. While Remer's model was specifically developed for adult rape trauma, the model is applicable for understanding survivors of child sexual abuse as well. This model attempts to integrate the rape experience and provide a positive involvement of the individual's strengths and coping strategies. This allows the victim to survive and enables her to resolve the rape, disclose it to others, and help other rape victims by offering social activism to bring about social changes related to rape and abuse.

SCURFIELD'S STRESS MANAGEMENT REDUCTION MODEL

Scurfield (1985) identifies a six-stage model addressing defense mechanisms and coping strategies for trauma survivors. It stresses the importance of facilitating recapitulation and reexperiencing of the trauma in the here-and-now. The model involving stages that address therapeutic trust, exploration of previous coping behaviors, recapitulation of the trauma, integration of the trauma and emotional catharsis, and survivor strategies that include personal responsibility, understanding of personal control, guilt, fear, shame, and other components of traumatization, provide for a clinical theory of abuse process and therapeutic intervention.

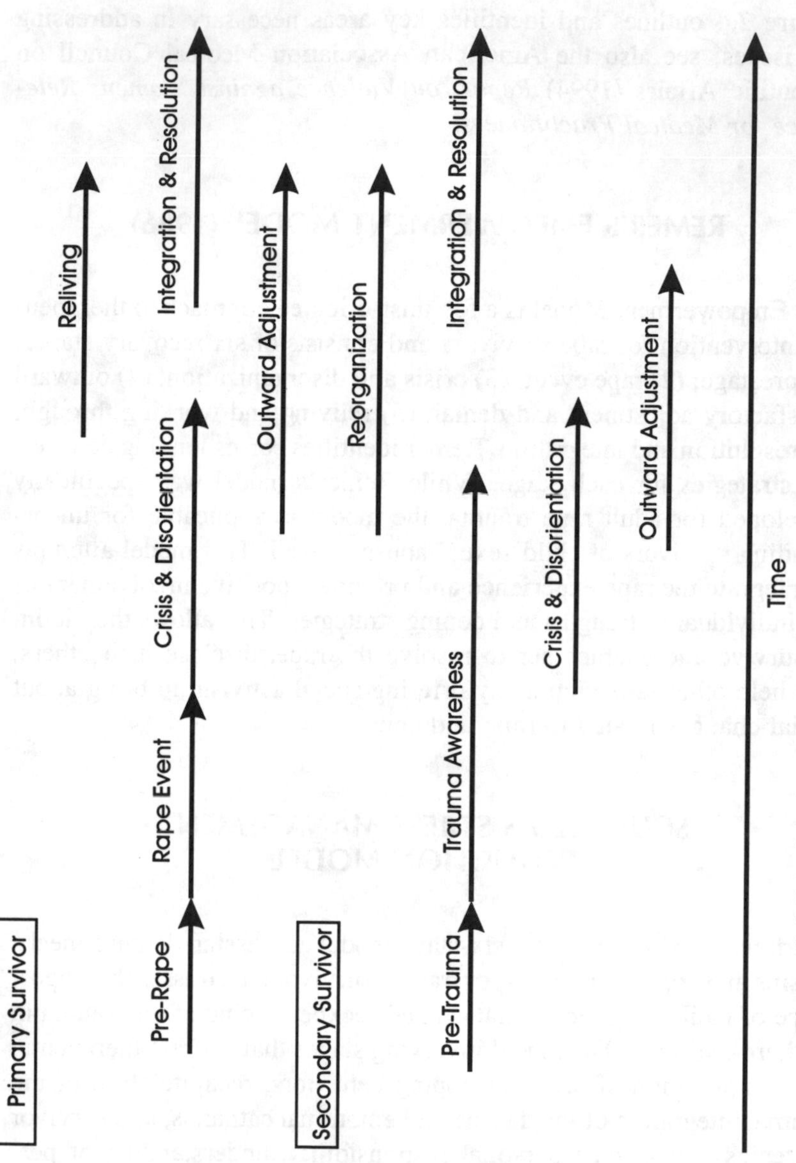

Figure 2.4 Interface between the healing processes of primary and secondary survivors

EPIDEMIOLOGICAL STUDIES

Evidence collected over the past two decades indicates that physical and sexual violence against women has grown steadily as a significant problem in health care delivery. Much of the violence is perpetrated by women's intimate partners or in relationships that would be presumed to carry some protective element. The violence carries with it both short- and long-term sequelae and affects both the victim's physical and psychological well-being. High prevalence rates of violence against women bring them into regular contact with physicians. At least one in five women is seen in emergency rooms with symptoms consistent with traumatization and abuse. Physicians, however, frequently treat the injuries only symptomatically and fail to recognize that the patient is a victim of physical or sexual abuse. Even when recognized, physicians often fail to address the needs of abused women.

Prevalence studies, using epidemiological methods, suggest that at least 20 percent of adult women, (7) depression; 15 percent of college-age women, and 12 percent of adolescent girls experience sex ual abuse during their lifetimes. The Human Abuse Prevention Council (1994) indicates that 25 percent of all girls under 18 and 18 percent of all boys under 18 have experienced some level of sexual abuse. Eighty-five percent of sexual assaults on children are committed by someone the child knows and usually trusts: an immediate family member, a friend, a relative, a neighbor. Sexual abuse happens when an adult or an older child uses a younger child for sexual stimulation. The medium by which stimulation is realized can vary from sexual fondling to handling of the genitals to attempted penetration or oral sex or actual intercourse. The perpetrators are more often male than female and there is little data to say whether this behavior is unique to any age, income class, or educational group. While it is estimated that one in six boys is sexually abused, the likelihood is rare that such a child would report the abuse, in part because of a fear that someone will accuse them of wrongdoing. This in turn leads them to a sexual abuse accommodation syndrome (Summit, 1983, see Figure 2.5).

The cycle of abuse can be broken. Children should be encouraged to know the difference between behavior that is right and behavior

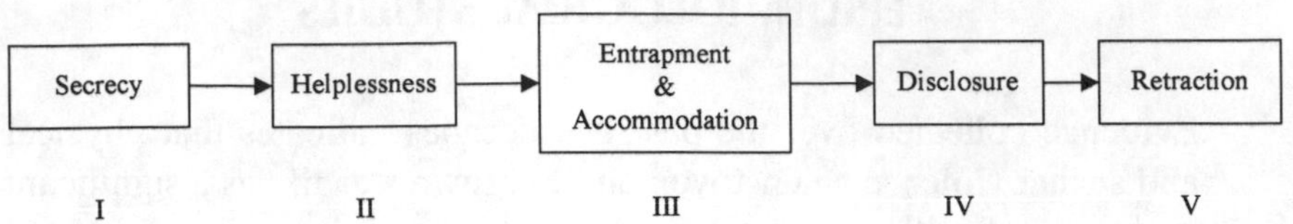

Figure 2.5 Sexual Abuse Accommodation Syndrome (Summit, 1983)

that is wrong, whether by an older child or an adult. This can help prevent abusive acts from taking place because children will have been alerted to the danger signals of sexually inappropriate behavior on the part of others. Among the most important factors is that a child should be encouraged to trust his or her own feelings of discomfort no matter who the person might be.

DATING ABUSE

Dating abuse is much more common than is often realized and is estimated to be present in some form in better than 17 to 22 percent of all dating relationships. Often at the core of dating abuse are unrealistic expectations on the part of one or both parties. Frustration leads to anger, and anger leads to abuse. Indicators often present include possessiveness, secrecy, isolation, need for control, dishonesty, lack of trust, and poor communication. Addressing issues of dating abuse requires recognition of refusal on the part of the victim of abuse (i.e., that "no" means "no" not "maybe") and abiding by a bill of rights which help to define the parameters of the relationship itself.

ELDER ABUSE

Statistics vary, but it is estimated that more than 25 percent of the elderly experience some level of abuse by their children, spouse, or external caregivers. Recent prevalent studies suggested that as many as 32 out of every 1000 people age 65 or older are abused. Physical violence has emerged as the most widespread form of maltreatment. The severity of reported violent incidents varies from 45 percent of the victims of physical violence who had something thrown at them, 63 percent who were pushed, 42 percent who were shoved or grabbed, and 10 percent who were hit or kicked. Although the physical abuse varied in intensity, it is clear that there is a growing recognition of elder abuse. Similar studies have suggested that, of the perpetrators, 58 percent were spouses, compared to 24 percent who were children. The elderly find themselves trapped in situations where they are intimidated and incapacitated. Elder abuse includes physical abuse, active neglect, passive neglect, psychological abuse, and financial abuse. Abuse of the elderly occurs because of the increased challenges of caring for frail and dependent people. With deteriorating health, the demands for care grow larger; as the stress increases, so does the likelihood of abuse. There are several important ingredients that can go into guarding the safety and well-being of elderly human beings.

Recognition of early signs and symptoms of elder abuse are critical to providing for the safety and well-being of elderly human beings. Among the most significant areas are (see also Table 1.2):

- Physical and/or sexual abuse (bruises, lacerations, fractures, venereal disease, pain or itching, bleeding of external genitalia, vaginal or anal areas)
- Psychological abuse (insults, threats, harassment, withholding of security and affection)
- Exploitation (misuse of income or financial resources; vulnerable elderly may show fear, depression, confusion, anger, and ambivalence)
- Medical abuse (improper administration or withholding of medications or necessary medical care that may result in confusion, disorientation, agitation, self-neglect)
- Neglect (failure to provide care necessary to maintain the physical and mental well-being of the person as manifested by poor personal hygiene, malnutrition, or other indicators)

The cycle of violence from generation to generation is often at the core of abusive caregivers and elderly victims of abuse. Multigenerational abuse of the elderly perpetuates itself when perpetrators fail to prepare themselves for the demands of caregiving to the elderly, for example, evaluating one's own ability to provide continuity of care to an elderly family member. There are also important issues related to irritating behaviors and multiple problems that deal with health, cognitive abilities, and behavioral change noted and accepted in the elderly person. Often a caregiver who loses control is ignoring his or her own needs, which must be met before an individual can give adequate care to others.

Utilizing multiple supports in a network that involves individuals and community based agencies is seen as essential in effectively providing care to the elderly and active prevention–intervention efforts in decreasing the level of physical and emotional abuse of the elderly.

IMPLICATIONS FOR CLINICAL PRACTICE

The clinician who has a clear understanding of the various clinical theories of adult abuse is better able to more adequately understand the complexity and clinical pathway of trauma. Theoretical consideration must be understood within the context of the victim–victimizer spectrum, as well as the following issues important in the care and management of the victim:

Objectives for Treating Abuse

1. Identify the abused person by noting both physical and behavioral indicators. Some will complain directly about the assault, while others exhibit various physical and emotional symptoms.
2. Manage the acute medical problems of the patient, including physical injury, venereal disease, and pregnancy. Learn to ask the "right" questions that enable the abused person to provide information that will enable you to help them.
3. Obtain and record an accurate history of the assault, including the answers to the questions of who, when, what, where, and how.
4. Manage the acute emotional problems of the patient and family resulting from the assault itself, the act of disclosure, police involvement, and the medical exam. These problems are often exacerbated by mixed feelings of anger, guilt, and frustration.

5. Safeguard the patient against further abuse by determining whether she or he is under unusual risk for abuse and needs to be placed in temporary custody.
6. Formulate treatment follow-up plans for the medical and emotional well-being of the patient.
7. Comply with the legal requirements for collection of evidence, documentation, and, depending upon the laws of the particular state, reporting of the assault as a crime.

These objectives are best achieved through a multidisciplinary effort involving health and mental health care providers, the criminal justice system, child and adult protective service agencies, and social support agencies.

3

Assessment of Abuse and Trauma: Clinical Measures

Abuse and traumatization of children and adults has encouraged careful attention to the measurement and evaluation of victimization across the abuse spectrum. Recent research addressing the negative psychological impact of abuse suggests correlates with posttraumatic stress disorder (PTSD), and, in the DSM-IV diagnostic entities (APA, 1994a), acute stress disorder with symptoms of flashbacks, nightmares, dissociation, and sleep disturbance being most prominent (Briere and Runtz, 1989; Putnam, 1989; Miller and Veltkamp, 1993).

Since the mid-1980s, a special effort has been made to develop psychometrically acceptable measures. The following instruments include but are not limited to, current measures seen as having been developed specifically to address the abuse syndrome and they demonstrate a sensitivity to abuse-specific conditions.

MEASURES USED TO ASSESS ADULT ABUSE VICTIMS

- Trauma Symptom Inventory (Briere and Runtz, 1989): This measure is a brief abuse-oriented instrument of psychometric quality that is used in clinical research as a measure of traumatic impact. It is considered for use in assessing the long-term effects of child abuse. The TSC-33 yields five subscale scores including the following: (1) anxiety; (2) depression; (3) dissociation; (4) postsexual abuse trauma; and (5) sleep disturbance. The measure yields a total score and has been shown to demonstrate both validity and reliability in a variety of studies (Bagley, 1989; Briere and Runtz, 1989; Megana, 1990; Williams, 1994). Identified weaknesses in the TSC-33 include: (1) the sleep disturbance subscale has limited reliability (alpha = .66); (2) there is some ambiguity regarding the content validity of the postsexual abuse trauma-hypothesized subscale (PSAT-H), which is seen as a measure of sexual abuse trauma; (3) there is no subscale within the TSC-33 that measures sexual difficulties, despite the prominence of such symptoms in adults molested as children.
- *The Rape Trauma Symptom Rating Scale* (RTSRS; DiVasto, Kaufman, and Jackson, 1980): The RTSRS was developed to assess the impact and symptoms related to rape trauma. Symptoms for this instrument were based on the Rape Trauma Syndrome (R. L. Burgess, 1979). These symptoms are predominantly depressive in nature, although elements of fear and anxiety are also present to a significant degree. Other symptoms that have been noted include somatic symptoms; change in jobs, residence, or school; self-blame, and difficulties in relationships with significant others. Eight separate scales are recognized in the Rape Trauma Symptom Rating Scale including: (1) sleep disorders; (2) appetite; (3) phobias; (4) motor behavior; (5) relationships; (6) self-esteem; (7) depression; (8) somatic reactions. Each are rated on a five-point Likert-type scale. This instrument has several potential applications for work with rape victims. It can be used to chart progress over time in measuring specific symptoms with target groups or as a means of comparing differing victim populations. It provides a guide for thorough inquiry into the sequelae of sexual assault.

- *Impact of Events Scale* (IES; Horowitz, Wilner, and Alvarez, 1979): The IES is an 11-item scale that has been used primarily as an adult measure, although this measure has childhood PTSD applications. The instrument includes subscales for intrusion and avoidance-numbing and is often used as a measure of post-traumatic stress disorder, according to generalized criteria.
- *The Structured Event Probe and Narrative Rating Scale* (SEPRATE; Dohrenwend, Raphael, Schwartz, Stueve, and Skodol, 1993): The SEPRATE provides a unique methodology for assessing stressful life experiences. This is a clinical interview and includes an events checklist and probes to obtain detailed information from the victim on the number, dates, and types of stressful life experiences.
- *Clinically Administered PTSD Scale* (CAPS-II; Blake, Wethers, Nagy, and Friedman, 1993): This is a structured clinical interview designed to assess 17 symptoms of posttraumatic stress disorder according to the DSM-IV (APA, 1994a). This is based on the original clinically administered PTSD scale and has been refined to provide a more accurate means of evaluating the frequency and intensity of dimensions of each symptom, the impact of the symptoms on the patient, social and occupational functioning, and the overall severity of the symptom complex.
- *The Impact of Events Scale-Revised* (IES-Rev.; Horowitz, Wilner, and Alvarez, 1979): This scale is a 20-item inventory which focuses on the assessment of intrusions and avoidance-numbing responses. It assesses the psychological consequences of exposure to traumatic events. With this 20-item scale, the subject enters the specific stressful life event being rated, estimating for each item the frequency of his or her experience over the past week on a 6-point Likert-type scale from "not at all" to "often." A score for each item is obtained, assigning the weights of 0, 1, 3, and 5 to the frequency categories. The time period of the previous week is used, because it was found to provide the most clinically valid reports of a person's current response levels. The instrument permits comparison of the impact of different kinds of life events and individual differences in response to these events. The revised IES reports a split-half reliability of .96 internal consistency of subscales calculating a

Cronbach's alpha for intrusion (.79), avoidance (.82). A correlation of R = .42 (t < 0.0002) between intrusion and avoidance subscales indicates that the two subscales were associated but did not measure identical dimensions.

- *The Dissociative Disorders Interview Schedule* (DDIS: Ross, Heber, Norton, Anderson, D., Anderson, G., and Barchett, 1989): DDIS is a structured interview utilizing DSM diagnostic criteria for dissociative disorders, somatization disorder, major depressive episode, and borderline personality disorder. Additional items provide information about substance abuse, child physical and sexual abuse, and secondary features of multiple personality disorder. Information gained from this measure provides information helpful in the differential diagnosis of dissociative disorders. The DDIS has an overall integrated reliability of .68. For a diagnosis of multiple personality disorder, it has specificity of 100 percent and a sensitivity of 90 percent. The measure possesses 131 questions, yielding 16 separate diagnostic scales.
- *Knowledge of Sexual Abuse Questionnaire* (KSAQ; Hibbard and Zollinger, 1990): This is a 14-item inventory assessing knowledge of sexual abuse issues. Questions are adapted from hazard studies on professional responses to child abuse. Specifically selected items assess knowledge of facts about reporting, dynamics, epidemiology, medical and psychological sequelae, and legal issues in child sexual abuse.
- *Jackson Incest Blame Scale* (JIBS; Jackson and Muttal, 1993): This is a 20-item self-report measure that assesses multidimensional aspects of attribution of blame in incest. Four constructs measured include victim, offender, societal, and situational blame. Five items are used to determine the degree to which subjects attribute blame for childhood sexual abuse to victims. Items are scored on a 6-point Likert scale. High scores represent greater attribution of victim blame. Internal consistency reliability coefficients for the JIBS range from .63 to .80.
- *Trauma Symptom Checklist-40* (TSC-40; Briere and Runtz, 1992): The 40-item inventory assesses traumatization and has five subscales, similar to the TSC-33. The five subscales include: (1) anxiety; (2) depression; (3) dissociation; (4) postsexual abuse

trauma; and (5) sleep disturbances. The measure yields a total score and has been shown to be an improved measure, both from the validity and reliability perspective over the TSC-33. The coefficient for the complete checklist is .89, with mean internal consistency for the six scales at .71. Validation studies undertaken with the TCS-40 (Elliot and Briere, 1992) have suggested that certain forms of abuse, may, for example, produce elevated depression scores while other forms or combinations of abuse may result in elevated sexual problem scores. Seven validation studies have examined the performance of the TSC-40 in discriminating abused from nonabused subjects. Results suggest that the TSC-40 scores appear to increase with individuals who have reported a history of both physical and sexual abuse. Elliot and Briere have suggested that the scores attained on the PSC-40 may be elevated as a result of various forms of victimization.

- *Incident Report Interview* (IRI; Kilpatrick, 1987): The IRI attempts to comprehensively assess lifetime history via a variety of crime events, utilizing the DSM-IV stressor criteria for PTSD. Eight areas are examined, including attempted rape, attempted or completed molestation, sexual assault, aggravated assault, robbery, and burglary. A behavioral definition is offered for each of these classifications of cases. The measure includes comprehensive instructions for a somewhat complex procedure for reducing information about multiple crime history into a final classification of up to three major indices of stressful life events. Specific crime characteristics includes age of onset, brief open-ended descriptions, reporting to police, serial versus single incident occurrences, relationship to the perpetrator, presence of a weapon, and reported fear of death or serious injury due to the stressful life event.
- *National Women's Study PTSD Module* (NWSPTSDM; Kilpatrick, Resnick, Saunders, and Best, 1989): This measure utilizes the PTSD module and contains comprehensive assessment of crime and direct assault events adapted from the Incident Report Interview (IRI; Kilpatrick, 1987). Similar to the IRI, each preface for the trauma assessment sections includes the sections for assessment for rape, molestation, attempted sexual assault, aggravated assault, with or without a weapon, and a separate

section covering criterion A events, including homicide, death, disaster, accident, witnessing violence, and other events that were perceived as life-threatening or that led to physical injury or damage. The National Women's Study PTSD Module provides assessment of multiple traumatic events and detailed information gathered about each subset of events.

- *Potential Stressful Events Interview* (PSE; Kilpatrick, Resnick, and Freedy, 1991): The potential Stressful Events Interview utilizes DSM-IV criteria and a subset of detailed questions adapted from the SCID-NP (Spitzer, Williams, and Gibbons, 1987). The interview consists of five components, including demographic characteristics, low magnitude stressors, high magnitude stressors, objective and subjective characteristics of recent stressful life experiences, and subjective reactions, including a self-report measure of emotional and physical responses which occurred at the time of the event. This is an extensive interview, and the PSE often takes a considerable amount of time to administer, particularly to a person who is being assessed following an extensive traumatization experience. A streamlined version, using both an interview and self-report format, entitled *Trauma Assessment for Adults,* is being developed (Resnick, Best, Kilpatrick, Freedy, and Falsetti, 1993).
- *Traumatic Stress Schedule* (TSS; Norris, 1990): The Traumatic Stress Schedule is a brief screening measure designed to provide basic information regarding the occurrence of traumatic events. It assesses a broad range of events, including death of a close friend or loved one, robbery, physical assault, sexual assault, motor vehicle crash, combat, fire, and disaster or other natural traumatic experiences. The reliability of the instrument is reported by the author as .88 for 10 trauma events, with a tendency for people to report more events in the first session than in the second session. Reliability for the PTSD items was also quite favorable, ranging from .74 for nonanchored items to .86 for anchored items. The instrument fails to identify trauma related features, such as life-threat experiences, which other researchers have found to be an important component in assessing the impact of stressful life events on health.

- *Traumatic Stress Institute Life Events Questionnaire* (TSI; MacIan and Perlman, 1992): The TSI is a 19-item self-report questionnaire embracing a broad range of stressful life experiences. It asks the client to rate the level of distress on a high–low dimension for both the time of the experience and the present. Examples of stressful life experiences include: domestic violence, neglect, physical abuse, sexual abuse, natural disasters, threatening illness, litigation, rape, war and military experiences, and other traumatic events.
- *Trauma History Questionnaire* (THQ; Green, 1990): The THQ utilizes DSM-IV criteria in a self-report format consisting of 24 items (APA, 1994a). It assesses a range of traumatic events, including crime-related events, general disaster and trauma, and physical and sexual assault. Test–retest reliability correlations show considerable variability depending on category, and range from .91 to .47.
- *PTSD Symptom Scale-Interview* (PSS-I; Foa, Riggs, Dancer, and Rothbaum, 1993): This is a 17-item semistructured interview that can be administered by trained interviewers. Each item corresponds to the 17 diagnostic criteria for PTSD according to DSM-IV (APA, 1994a). The interview rates each item on a 4-point Likert-type scale. The total severity score is calculated as a sum of the severity ratings for the 17 items. High test–retest reliability, satisfactory internal consistency, and good concurrent validity are reported. The interview version yielded a high interrater agreement when administered separately by two interviewers, and excellent convergent validity with the SDI of DSM-IV.

MEASURES USED TO ASSESS PERPETRATOR CHARACTERISTICS

- *Child Abuse Potential Inventory* (CAP; Milner, 1980): The CAP inventory is a screening device that measures a person's potential for physically abusing a child. The CAP attempts to measure parental pathology, as well as interactional difficulties that are related to physical child abuse. The CAP inventory asks subjects to agree or disagree with statements that have been made to discriminate between physical abusers and nonabusers. Factors derived from the abuse scale describe psychological difficulties such as stress, rigidity and unhappiness in interpersonal problems, problems with child and self, with family, and problems perceived as deriving from others. Validity and reliability data reveal that the CAP abuse scale reliability (KR-20) ranges from .91 to .96 for a variety of control, at risk neglect and abuse groups, and test–retest reliabilities from .91 to .75 for control subjects across one day, one week, one month, and three-month intervals, respectively. The CAP abuse score has been found to correlate significantly with psychological factors such as external locus of control, poor ego strength, life hassles, life stress, depression, and anxiety, and tension, and instability.

- *The Child Care Attitude Inventory* (CAI; Jones and Fay, 1988): This 80-item inventory is designed to assess adults' potential for providing quality child care as opposed to neglectful and abusive care. The inventory is a paper-and-pencil measure, which measures a number of attitudes and emotional states that have been differentiated between adults who have healthy, constructive interactions with children from adults who have unhealthy, destructive interactions (Jones and Fay, 1988). A 5-point Likert-type type scale, ranging from 1 to 5, is used in the assessment of child care attitudes. The specific dimensions measured by this scale include (1) emotional stability; (2) expectations of children; (3) tolerance of attitudes toward child abuse; (4) explanations of child abuse. A factor analyzed study confirmed the presence of four specific factors, a Spearman-Brown split half (odd vs. even) reliability coefficient realized .91. The CCAI has shown a relationship effect with the Child Abuse Potential Inventory ($R = -.88$, $P < .001$), suggesting that adults with better child care potential exhibited lower child abuse potential.
- *Multiphasic Sex Inventory* (Nichols and Molinder, 1984). This measure is used in assessing treatment progress and therapy outcome of the perpetrator of child sex abuse. It is a 300-item

measure requiring a true or false answer. It possesses an MMPI-type format and includes a 50-item sex history. The MSI has 20 scales, 6 of which are validity scales assessing the client's attitude at the time of taking the test. The remaining 14 scales include a variety of sexual deviance measures, a sexual knowledge and belief measure, a measure of sexual dysfunction, and an assessment of motivation and treatment. The authors report a Kudor-Richardson reliability for only three scales, which were .71, .65, and .40, respectively, on the social–sexual desirability, sexual obsessions, and sexual knowledge scales. Pearson product moment correlations of stability over time range from .58 to .92, with the majority of them in the .80 range or higher. The test–retest correlations for the entire MSI was reported to be .89.

CONCLUSION

The Diagnostic and Statistical Manual (DSM-IV; APA, 1994a) has recognized new criteria that aid in conceptualizing traumatization and stress. The measures herein defined, aid in our understanding of this syndrome of both acute traumatic stress disorder and posttraumatic stress disorder, as defined by the DSM-IV. We must, however, recognize that traumatization shows itself in different ways in each individual and over time. The symptom clusters that emerge include the following:

1. Depression. Mood swings and inability or unwillingness to address the effects of the trauma often result in both episodic and chronic depressive features.
2. Anxiety. Apprehensive expectations, anticipatory anxiety, motor tension, and autonomic hyperactivity, vigilance, and scanning are clearly recognized.
3. Obsessive–compulsive behavior. The experience of stressful life events often results in intense feelings of helplessness and hopelessness. The pervasive loss of control leads individuals to regain that control through obsessive and compulsive activities, resulting in an artificial sense of security.

Table 3.1 Instruments for the Assessment of Abuse

Instrument	General Classification	Description	Special Features
Measures Used to Assess Adult Abuse Victims			
Trauma Symptom Checklist-33 (Briere & Runtz, 1989)	Self-report	33 items with 5 subscales measuring sleep disturbances, depression, and dissociation	A post-sexual-abuse subscale is included in this measure
Rape Trauma Symptom Rating Scale (RTSRS) (DiVasto, 1985)	Self-report	8 subscales rated on 5-point Likert-type scale to access impact of rape	Measures both symptoms and adaptation to trauma
Impact of Events Scale (Horowitz et al., 1979)	Self-report	11 items yield total score assessing impact of trauma	Includes subscales for intrusion and avoidance-numbing
Structured Event Probe and Narrative Rating Scale (Dohrenmend, et al., 1993)	Clinical interview	Structured interview with ratings for severity of impact stressful events	Includes an events checklist
Clinically Administered PTSD Scale (Blake et al., 1990)	Clinical interview	Assesses the DSM criteria for PTSD	Refined over version 1 to assess frequency and intensity rating
Impact of Events Scale-Revised (Horowitz et al., 1979)	Self-report	Revised 20-item scale measuring consequences of exposure to trauma	Measures frequency and intensity of exposure
Dissociative Disorders Interview Schedule (Ross et al., 1989)	Structured clinical interview	DSM criteria for dissociation, depression, borderline personality disorder	Assesses substance abuse, child physical and sexual abuse history

Table 3.1 *(continued)*

Instrument	General Classification	Description	Special Features
Knowledge of Sexual Abuse Questionnaire (Hibbard & Zollinger, 1990)	Self-report	14-item inventory assessing knowledge of sexual abuse	Assesses knowledge of facts about reporting and legal issues
Jackson Incest Blame Scale (Jackson & Muttal, 1993)	Self-report	20-item inventory assessing aspects of attribution of blame in incest	Internal consistency reliability coefficients range as high as .80
Trauma Symptom Checklist 40 (Briere & Runtz, 1992)	Self-report	40-item measures with 5 subscales to assess traumatization	Improved validity and reliability date over TSC-33 version
Incident Report Interview (IRI) (Kilpatrick, 1987)	Clinical interview	Assesses 8 areas of trauma using DSM-IV stressor criteria	Specific crime characteristics are included in the measure
National Women's Study PTSD Module (Kilpatrick et al., 1989)	Clinical interview	Utilizes PTSD DSM criteria	Assesses multiple traumatic events
Potential Stressful Events Interview (Kilpatrick et al., 1991)	Clinical interview	DSM-IV criteria for PTSD and questions adapted from DSM SCID	Assesses high magnitude stressors
Traumatic Stress Schedule (TSS) (Norris, 1990)	Brief screening	Assesses broad range of events	Good reliability estimates noted
Traumatic Stress Institute Life Events Questionnaire (MacIan & Perlman, 1992)			

Table 3.1 Instruments for the Assessment of Abuse *(continued)*

Instrument	General Classification	Description	Special Features
Trauma History Questionnaire (Green, 1990)	Self-report	Utilizes DSM IV criteria within the 24-item measure	Test–retest reliability shows wide variability depending on category
Measures Used to Assess Perpetrator Characteristics			
Child Abuse Potential Inventory (CAP) (Milner, 1980)	Brief screening measure	Measures a previous potential for physical abuse	Assesses perpetration pathology
The Childcare Attitude Inventory (Jones & Fay, 1988)	Self-report	80-item inventory to assess abuse and neglect; uses 5-point Likert scale	Assesses emotional stability and attitudes of caregiver
The Multiphasic Sex Inventory (Nichols & Molinder, 1984)	Objective self-report measure	300-item inventory with MMPI-type format	Includes a 50-item sexual history scale

4. Dissociation–dissociative qualities are often recognized in individuals with a diagnosis of PTSD and can be associated as a result of experiencing the traumatizing events. Dissociation further shows itself through memory loss and avoidance types of behaviors in the victim.

Multiaxial assessment of life stress events that include criteria developed by the American Psychiatric Association through the DSM-IV, together with measures of the psychological components of post-traumatic stress disorder, become core ingredients in our growing understanding and our ability to more effectively diagnose and treat this disorder. Efforts to carefully assess the onset and etiology of traumatization must also address its compounding problems and premorbid factors. Our efforts to carefully understand the etiology of this disorder, assess biochemical imbalance, genetic abnormalities, and personality characteristics, seem extremely important to our growing knowledge. Reviewed herein are several recently developed measures that provide well-structured, clinical interviews based on definitional criteria from the nomenclature of the DSM-IV and the classification of disorders. Such measures will help to enhance and improve the validity and reliability of diagnostic examination measures important in the study of PTSD and its treatment. What is clear is the increase in clinicians' awareness of the impact of stressful life experiences and the resulting traumatization. These measures not only serve as an initial diagnostic medium, but also as a measure of change over time. Recent research has found that PTSD is primarily linked to stressful experiences and is more associated with these experiences than any of the other anxiety-related disorders.

4

The Medical Evaluation of Adult Victims of Abuse

Gary W. Kearl, M.D., M.S.P.H.

INTRODUCTION

Domestic Violence has been defined as any method employed to exert power and control by one individual over another in an adult relationship. It may take the form of physical abuse, sexual abuse, economic control, or social isolation of the victim. It includes behavior that physically harms (punching, slapping, pulling hair, kicking, punching, stabbing or shooting); arouses fear (threatening, intimidating, or using a threatening facial expression as a weapon); prevents the individual from doing as he or she wishes (dressing in certain clothes, seeking an education, obtaining employment, seeing family or friends); or forces the individual to behave in a certain way. *Psychological Abuse* can include any form of nonphysical harassment which exerts control of the individual through shame, humiliation, or denigration (Holtz, Esposito, and Podhorin, 1994, p. 848). *Elder Abuse* includes physical, sexual, and psychological abuse; as well as the withholding of food, clothing, and medical care. Some have also defined *financial exploitation* as a form of elder abuse (AMA, 1987, p. 967).

Although domestic violence may result in serious injuries, the severity of the abuse is poorly correlated with the extent of the resulting physical injuries. Accordingly, if health care providers only rely upon the presence of physical injuries to diagnose abuse, many victims of domestic violence will remain undetected (Holtz, Esposito et al., 1994, p. 848).

Populations at Increased Risk for Domestic Violence

It is estimated that 3 to 4 percent of adult men and women experience at least one episode of severe violence (injury from beating or from use of a knife or gun) per year (Gelles, 1987, pp. 37–39). Although victims are not restricted to any demographic group, female sex is the single strongest risk factor for becoming an adult victim of abuse (Holtz et al., 1994, p. 848). Moreover, certain types of patients seem to be more vulnerable to abuse than others.

Adolescents

Rates of abuse are difficult to quantify for this age group. It is estimated that over 700,000 women are raped each year and that 61 percent of these victims are under the age of 18 (American Academy of Pediatrics, 1995, p. 761). Adolescents who leave home at an early age may be fleeing from an abusive relationship in the home (Farber, Kinast, McCoard, 1984, p. 298) or may fall into an abusive relationship while living on the street. Moreover, violence within sexually intimate relationships seems to be more common among adolescent women than among older women (AAP, 1995, p. 761).

Pregnant Females

Although pregnancy is often portrayed as a ''happy'' time for women, literature on battered women suggest that 25 to 63 percent experienced battering while they were pregnant (Helton, McFarlane, and Anderson, 1987, p. 1337).

Elderly

Many elderly eventually become incapable of caring for themselves. As a result, they are particularly vulnerable to willful neglect as well as abuse. It is estimated that 3 percent of elderly adults suffer from abuse or neglect each year (Lachs and Fulmer, 1993, p. 667).

Responsibilities of Health Care Providers

Health care providers have a responsibility to provide adult victims of abuse or assault with:

Diagnosis of the "problem"
Emotional support
Medical assessment and treatment of injuries
Prevention of pregnancy
Documentation of the alleged assault by collection of evidence for police
Referral to appropriate counseling services
Expert medical testimony in subsequent litigation

PROBLEMS IN EVALUATING VICTIMS OF ABUSE

The physician's task of evaluating suspected abuse victims is complicated by several problems which are unique to adult abuse:

1. *Physician unwillingness to intervene.* A recent study of primary care physicians (Sugg and Innui, 1992, p. 3157) identified factors which decrease physician willingness to identify and/or intervene in cases of domestic violence. These include: inadequate time during practice to screen for cases of domestic violence; lack of training in diagnosis and treatment of victims of domestic violence; fear of offending victims of domestic violence; feelings of powerlessness to stop domestic violence; inability to believe that domestic violence is taking

place among patients in the practice; and fear that intervening in cases of domestic violence will create worse problems for the victim. *Health care providers must attempt to rectify personal factors which make them unable or unwilling to identify and intervene in cases of adult abuse.*

2. *Masked Abuse.* Many victims of abuse are unable to seek medical care because of the controlling nature of their relationship with the abuser. Moreover, abused adults with diminished mental capacity may not recognize when they are being victimized by their caregivers. *Accordingly, health care providers who care for adults most remain open to this diagnostic possibility and engage in active case finding during routine medical evaluations.*

3. *Strain on the Family System.* Many victims are abused by a relative or close acquaintance. As a result, the family system may become so strained by a revelation of abuse that the perpetrator of the abuse may actually be protected by persons within the family circle who would normally be responsible for protecting the victim. In such instances, the victim may either be blamed for the abusive incident or his or her story may be vigorously denied. *Consequently, health care personnel should be prepared to assist abused adults to obtain alternative sources of emotional support.*

4. *Cyclic Abuse.* Many victims are abused in a cyclic fashion with intervening periods of "more satisfactory" relations with the perpetrator of the abuse. As a result, victims may be reluctant to seek medical care following an abusive incident in hopes that "things will get better." *Health care personnel must avoid negative judgments of abuse victims who seem reluctant to break off abusive relationships.*

5. *Delay in Seeking Care.* Many abuse victims do not seek medical care until some time after the event. Consequently, little or no physical evidence may be found to corroborate the victim's story. Because a lack of physical evidence may further reinforce denial on the part of the family, *it is critical that victims of abuse receive a thorough medical evaluation.*

6. *Difficulty in Protecting the Abuse Victim.* Unlike victims of child abuse, adult victims are *not* automatically placed in protective custody once abuse is disclosed. As a result, some adult victims may be reluctant to report abuse because of fears that the mere act of reporting past abuse will make them more vulnerable to another (even

more violent) cycle of abuse. *Accordingly, it is essential that health care personnel assist victims to find protective shelter once abuse has been revealed in order to protect them from more serious injuries as a result of having made the disclosure of abuse.*

MEDICAL EVALUATION OF ABUSED ADULTS

Abuse Evaluation Site

If a victim of abuse presents for a medical evaluation within 72 hours of the event, the examiner should be familiar with local forensic examination procedures. (State laws/guidelines usually govern the content of such examinations.) If the examiner is unsure of how to proceed, the victim should be referred to a medical facility (emergency room, rape crisis center, etc.) which is equipped to evaluate the victim's symptoms according to an appropriate forensic examination protocol. The examination should document the nature of the abuse, the full extent of any injuries, and the examiner should ensure that there is an unbroken (legal) "chain of evidence" for all forensic specimens collected during the course of the examination. ("Rape kits" may be obtained from police agencies to facilitate collection of forensic specimens.) If the victim presents for a medical evaluation more than 72 hours after the event, the victim should probably be examined in a physician's office. In this circumstance, the examination procedure is the same, but the examiner does not need to collect forensic specimens, since such specimens will no longer be present when more than 72 hours have elapsed since the abusive incident.

Evaluation of Abused Adults in the Emergency Room Setting

The emergency room is often the first point of contact with the health care system for adult victims of abuse. Although some victims present for care after reporting a history of abuse, others will seek medical care without revealing the cause of their symptoms. As a result, emergency room personnel must be prepared to evaluate obvious as well as *masked* cases of abuse. In recognition of this problem, the Joint Commission on Accreditation of Healthcare Organizations (JCAHO) has recommended that accredited emergency facilities develop and implement procedures for identifying and caring for adult victims of domestic violence (Scott and Matricciani, 1994, p. 892).

The emergency room is frequently chaotic and stressful to patients and medical personnel alike. Moreover, it is more difficult to maintain patient anonymity in this setting since there are more staff members in an emergency department than there are in a physician's office who are permitted routine access to medical records. As a result, special care must be taken to preserve patient anonymity and confidentiality of records when evaluating victims of abuse in this setting. In general, emergency medical personnel should remember:

Triage. Abuse victims should be identified and examined expeditiously.

Consent. All abuse evaluations should be conducted with the consent of the victim or the victim's legal guardian.

Chain of Custody. The evaluation should be conducted in a manner which safeguards the legal validity of forensic specimens.

Reporting. Adult protective authorities should be notified of the results of abuse evaluations.

Training. Each institution should conduct regular in-service training of emergency medical staff to ensure that victims of abuse are properly evaluated.

Evaluation of Abused Adults in the Primary Care Setting

Research suggests that 12 to 28 percent of adults presenting to primary care practices have experienced domestic violence (Gin, Rucker, Frayne, and Hibbard, 1991, p. 320). Moreover, domestic violence is the most common cause of trauma to women, and victims of domestic violence tend to utilize health services more frequently than adults who are not experiencing this type of stress (Holtz et al., 1994, p. 849). As a result, primary care practitioners should include ''case-finding'' questions when documenting the social history and should consider the possibility of domestic violence whenever the history does not logically account for the patient's symptoms-findings. Finally, continuity of care provided in primary care practices facilitates eventual reporting of abuse, particularly if the provider demonstrates an appropriate level of concern about family violence (Holtz et al., 1994, p. 850).

RESPONSIBILITIES OF OFFICE PERSONNEL

Patient Appointments

Adult victims of abuse should always be seen expeditiously. Even though cases may be identified weeks to months after the most recent abusive contact, a medical evaluation for suspected abuse should not be postponed, because delays in evaluating the victim increase the risk of more serious injury. As a result, adults, who seek medical care for symptoms suggestive of abuse, should be evaluated in sufficient detail during the first visit to ensure that they do not require emergency medical care and should be referred *during that visit* for social services and/or to the police so they can obtain protection from further abuse.

Office Environment

The physician should strive to create and maintain an office environment which encourages victims to disclose abuse. This can be accomplished by hanging posters on the subject of domestic violence or placing literature in locations (patient exam rooms or restrooms) where potential victims of abuse will be sure to see them. Such measures can send a message that it is "OK" to talk about abuse in this office.

Patient Registration

The office receptionist is responsible for expediting the registration process for suspected victims of abuse. Patient confidentiality is of special concern in these cases. It is particularly important to prevent the abuser (who may be the victim's spouse or close relative) from finding out that the victim has received a medical evaluation for symptoms of abuse because such a revelation may incite another cycle of abuse, before the victim can be fully protected. One way to maximize patient confidentiality is to prepare an abuse case folder that is filed in a separate location from the regular medical record. This folder can be used to hold sensitive case notes and is cross-referenced to the regular chart. In this way, any information pertaining to the evaluation for suspected abuse can be easily retrieved, yet routine scrutiny of the victim's regular medical chart will not automatically reveal sensitive examination data. When access to this information is requested from insurance carriers or other agencies, specific permission should be obtained from the patient.

Nursing Responsibilities

The nurse in attendance assists the examiner in performing the physical examination. The nurse should:

1. Prepare the room for the examination and place the following supplies in the exam room prior to the examination:
   Bright light source (e.g., goose-neck lamp)
   Magnification device (hand-held lens or magnifying loop, if available)
   Tape recorder and audiotapes (if the examiner wishes to record the interview)
   Tape measure (marked in millimeters)
   Camera to document any skin injuries.
2. Measure and record in the chart the patient's weight and temperature.
3. Completely label all laboratory specimens and verify with the examiner that each specimen container is properly marked *before leaving the exam room.*
4. Ensure that the laboratory specimens are expeditiously forwarded to an appropriate lab facility.

Interviewer/Examiner Responsibilities

The interviewer and the examiner are usually the same person. The interviewer is responsible for obtaining a history of the abuse. The examiner is responsible for performing the physical examination, and arranging for appropriate medical treatment for victims of abuse. In addition, the examiner should discuss the need for counseling services and make referrals to other specialists when appropriate. Both the interviewer and examiner should reassure the victim that the information obtained from the victim during the evaluation will *not* be shared with the perpetrator of the abuse. If the interviewer/examiner is the health care provider for the entire family, the victim's safety and well-being must take precedence over the family's needs, even when the perpetrator is a spouse or family member.

Medical History

Documentation of abuse is often completely dependent upon the history because many forms of adult abuse are psychological and do not leave physical signs. The interview should be conducted in a tactful yet thorough manner. Normally, the victim should be interviewed *privately.* Unwillingness of an accompanying partner to allow the victim to be interviewed alone should arouse concern in the interviewer's mind. In some instances victims may request that a support person remain with them during the interview. However, victims of abuse are often emotionally manipulated by their assailants. Moreover, victims are frequently threatened with physical harm in order to prevent them from disclosing details of the abuse. As a result, it is virtually impossible for a victim to make a straightforward disclosure of abuse when the perpetrator is present. If the interviewer becomes concerned that the person accompanying the victim is really the perpetrator of the abuse and is trying to maintain control over the victim during the medical evaluation, the interviewer should try to separate the suspected perpetrator of abuse from the victim and interview the victim alone.

When a victim has made a disclosure of abuse prior to the start of the medical evaluation, the interviewer should directly ask the victim to describe the nature of the abuse, including details as to: what happened; where it happened; when it happened; and who did it. The interviewer should avoid using terms such as *abused, battered,* or *domestic violence,* during the interview, because these terms may not mean the same thing to the victim and may cause the victim to leave out important details of the history.

If a patient presents with signs or symptoms suggestive of abuse but has not yet reported any history of abuse, the interviewer may begin by asking the patient: "How are things going in your family?" Alternatively, the interviewer may inquire as to how conflicts are resolved in the home and whether or not hitting is ever used as a means of conflict resolution. McFarlane has proposed three questions which may be used to screen pregnant women for abuse during routine prenatal visits (McFarlane, Parker, Soeken, 1992, p. 3177):

1. Within the past year, have you been hit, slapped, kicked, or otherwise physically hurt by someone?
2. Since you have become pregnant have you been hit, slapped, kicked, or otherwise physically hurt by someone?
3. Within the past year, has anyone forced you to have unwanted sexual activity?

The interviewer should remember the following points while interviewing the victim:

1. *Setting.* Arrange for a comfortable interview setting.
2. *Anxiety.* Maintain a relaxed atmosphere during the interview.
3. *Continuum of exposure.* Try to document both the duration and progression of the abuse over time.

Special Problems with Interviewing Victims of Sexual Abuse/Assault

Victims of sexual abuse frequently express a wide range of emotions during the interview. Such feelings should always be acknowledged and any underlying fears identified. Adult victims of sexual abuse-assault should be encouraged to describe what happened. The interviewer should ask the victim to point to *any* parts of his or her body which may have received sexual contact (e.g., mouth, breasts, genitals, anus, etc.). Information as to whether penetration occurred, and whether ejaculation took place should be sought and recorded. Finally, female victims of sexual abuse-assault should be asked about signs or symptoms of pregnancy.

The interviewer should conduct a review of systems which must include inquiry as to recent or past episodes of unexplained chronic pain, injuries, and suspicious behavioral signs/symptoms (Table 4.1).

THE PHYSICAL EXAMINATION—PRELIMINARY CONSIDERATIONS

Special Problems Associated with Examining Victims of Abuse/Assault

Victims of abuse may become very fearful during the evaluation process. Such feelings should always be acknowledged and any underlying fears identified and addressed by the examination personnel. Some female victims become frightened at the prospect of a pelvic examination because they fear the exam will be traumatic. The examiner can usually reassure such individuals by carefully explaining the nature of the examination. A frightened adult may be further persuaded to cooperate with the physical examination if another, supportive adult remains in the room during the examination and if the examiner proceeds slowly through the examination, explaining each step, and allowing the victim to have as much control over the progress of the examination as possible.

Physical Examination

The physical examination should include a careful inspection of the skin, head, and genitalia for signs of injury.

Skin

The skin is the largest organ of the body and the most vulnerable target of abuse. Cutaneous signs of abuse include multiple bruises in various stages of healing, burns (particularly in the central region of the body), and scratches. In addition, in situations where the patient has diminished mental capacity, the skin can reveal *masked abuse* through signs of poor hygiene (dirt, decubitus ulcers, etc.), dehydration (tenting of the skin, dryness of the lining of the mouth), malnutrition (loss of skin color and luster), and improper use of physical restraints (circumferential bruises around the wrists and ankles).

Table 4.1 Significant Signs and Symptoms from the Review of Systems

Multiple (unexplained) Injuries to the Central Region of the Body	Skin: Bruises, Scratches, Burns Head: Facial Bruises, Mandibular Fractures, Hearing Loss/Ruptured Tympanic Membranes Genitalia: Injury/Mutilation
Unexplained Chronic Pain	Recurrent Headaches, Abdominal Pain Pelvic Pain/Dyspareunia
Behavioral Signs/Symptoms	Depression: Suicidal ideation, weight loss, insomnia Anxiety: Palpitations, insomnia, agoraphobia Alcohol Abuse Pregnancy: Amenorrhea, Breast Enlargement, Morning Sickness

Head and Face

The examiner should look for the signs of abuse listed in Table 4.1. These may include signs of blows to the face (peri-orbital bruises, orbital fractures, mandibular fracture or disarticulation, swollen lips, or missing teeth); the scalp (hematomas or hair loss); the ears (fractured ear cartilage or ruptured tympanic membranes); and the neck (circumferential bruises from attempts at choking).

Anogenital Area

Although the external genitalia and anus may already demonstrate signs of healed trauma from past (consensual) sexual intercourse, the victim should still be examined for corroborating signs of recent physical or sexual abuse.

Female Genitalia

The examiner should inspect each part of the external genitalia including the labia majora, labia minora, clitoris, fossa navicularis, posterior fourchette, and periurethral and perihymenal mucosal surfaces; for signs of fresh injury (genital discharge, hyperpigmentation, bruising, laceration, burns, or bleeding).

Male Genitalia

Both the penis and the scrotum are potential targets of abuse. A complete description of the appearance of the penis including the location of any erythema, bruising, suction marks, excoriations, burns, or skin lacerations should be noted. Tenderness of the testicles or epididymis and urethral discharge are additional physical signs which may reflect evidence of traumatic injury. Particular care should be taken to rule out torsion of a painful testicle.

Anus

Anal penetration may occur without leaving any sign of physical injury. As a result, it is not unusual for the anus to have a "normal" appearance despite a history of anal abuse. The anal examination may be conducted in the lateral decubitus or the supine position (with the knees curled up toward the chest). The examiner should first inspect the buttocks and the perianal skin for bruising, hematomas, deep fissures, abrasions, lacerations, inflammation, thickening, and pigmentation changes. The anal sphincter of patients who have been sodomized may dilate abnormally during the course of the anal examination. Significant anal sphincter injury should be referred to a colorectal surgeon.

SPECIAL TECHNIQUES FOR EXAMINING VICTIMS OF SEXUAL ABUSE/ASSAULT

1. *Draping.* Adults almost always feel more comfortable when they are draped during the examination. The examiner should strive to maintain the modesty of the patient throughout the examination.
2. *Exposure of the genitalia for the exam.* Two standard examination techniques: *Labial Separation and Traction* are commonly used to expose the female genitalia during the physical examination. Labial

separation is obtained by placing thumbs on the labia majora and applying gentle pressure laterally and downward. Labial traction is produced by grasping the labia major and gently pulling them simultaneously downward and toward the examiner. *It is important to avoid creating iatrogenic physical abnormalities from the use of "heavy-handed" examination techniques during this phase of the physical examination.*

Figure 4.1 Vaginal Examination—*Labial Separation*

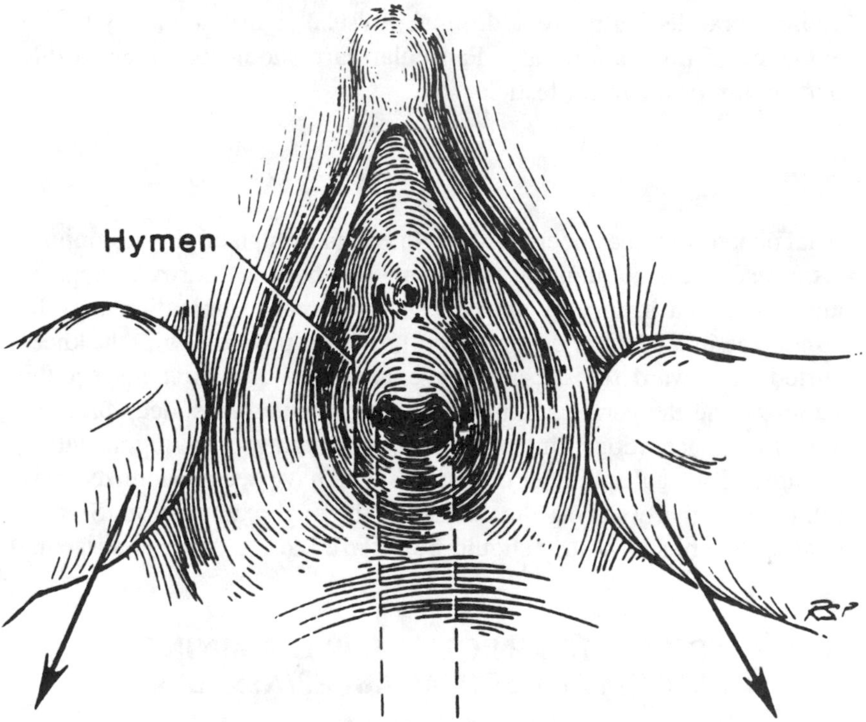

3. *Vaginal Speculum Examination* (see Figure 4.1). Female victims who report a history of sexual abuse should receive a speculum examination (including a Papanicolaou smear) to look for vaginal and cervical trauma.

4. *Anoscopy.* Sodomy victims should be examined with an anoscope to look for foreign bodies and signs of rectal trauma.

Sexually Transmitted Diseases

Culture samples for gonorrhea and chlamydia should be obtained from oropharynx, rectum, and the cervix of females. Males should be cultured for the same pathogens from the oropharynx, rectum, and urethra.

Culture Techniques for Sexually Transmitted Diseases

1. *Neisseria gonorrhea.* Cultures for gonorrhea should be plated directly onto a *warmed* transgrow medium and sent to the bacteriology lab within 30 minutes or placed in storage in a warmer set at 35 to 36°C. Rectal swabs for gonorrhea should be free of obvious fecal contamination since rectal flora will overgrow gonococcal organisms and possibly result in a false negative culture result. All positive gonorrhea cultures should be confirmed by a second independent biochemical test to avoid the possibility of a false positive culture result.

2. *Chlamydia trachomatis.* Chlamydia is an obligate intracellular bacterial pathogen which prefers to grow within the columnar epithelium of the ano–genital–urinary tract. Rapid antigen detection methods are *not* reliable for use in abuse evaluations. Accordingly, chlamydia cultures are the preferred method of diagnosing anogenital chlamydia infections in this population. Chlamydia is cultured by scraping epithelial cells directly from the suspected infection site with a sterile swab and quickly dropping the swab into a *cooled,* buffered transport solution. The transport solution should then be transported on ice to the lab.

3. *Human Papilloma Virus (HPV).* The human papilloma virus is the causative agent of cutaneous and genital warts (Condyloma acuminata). Studies of the HPV genome have identified more than 60 distinct subtypes of DNA. These studies have also confirmed that HPV lesions tend to be site specific and that anogenital warts are most frequently caused by HPV DNA subtypes 6, 11, 16, 18, 31, 33, and 35 (Ferenczy, 1995, p. 1332). Suspicious anogenital lesions can be soaked with a 3 or 5 percent solution of acetic acid and observed for "acetowhitening" of the epithelial surface (Pfenninger, 1989, pp. 287).

(Some victims may experience a burning or stinging sensation upon application of the acetic aid solution.) Unfortunately, acetowhitening is a nonspecific epithelial response. As a result, genital lesions which turn white in response to application of acetic acid should be tested for the presence of intracellular HPV DNA using one of several commercially available tests to confirm whether they actually represent HPV lesions of a type which are known to be sexually transmitted.

Although it is well accepted that anogenital HPV infections are transmitted through sexual contact, the long latency period (1 to 20 months) between initial infection and development of visible HPV lesions, makes a definitive determination of the source of genital warts in victims problematic. DNA typing studies of cutaneous/genital HPV lesions may become particularly helpful in clarifying the source of such infections in abuse cases.

4. *Human Immunodeficiency Virus (HIV).* The decision to screen for HIV infection is primarily dependent upon the victim's risk of contracting HIV during abusive contacts. Most adult rape victims will be tested for HIV. However, many adult victims of abuse may not be fully aware of their abuser's risk status. As a result, adult victims of abuse should be offered the chance to undergo HIV testing if they have had sexual contact with the perpetrator or have been exposed to blood during abusive incidents (Dwyer et al., 1993, p. 327).

5. *Other Sexually Transmitted Diseases.* The decision to screen for other STDs should be based upon the local prevalence of each STD (CDC, 1993a, 1–102).

Other Laboratory Tests

Additional laboratory testing (such as X rays, etc) should be ordered as indicated by the history or physical exam and the results recorded in the medical record.

INTERVENTIONS ON BEHALF OF VICTIMS OF ABUSE

Health care personnel must respond positively to adults who report abuse (Loring and Smith, 1994, p. 331). Failure to acknowledge the seriousness of the situation will increase the victim's sense of isolation and helplessness. The American Medical Association has developed "Diagnostic and Treatment Guidelines on Domestic Violence" (Flitcraft, 1992). Health care providers should:

Explicitly acknowledge the seriousness of the victim's situation.
Reaffirm that the victim has a right to feel safe from further abuse.

To this end, health care providers should help the victim to assess his or her current level of safety. Several factors are known to increase the risk of domestic violence ending in homicide (Campbell, 1994, p. 886):

1. Increasing frequency or severity of violence.
2. Presence of firearms in the home.
3. Coexisting sexual abuse.
4. Use of drugs or alcohol by the perpetrator.
5. Violent abuse occurring outside of the home.
6. Death threats from the perpetrator.
7. Attempts by the perpetrator to control all the aspects of the victim's life.
8. Expressions of violent jealousy by the perpetrator.
9. Battering during pregnancy.

If the victim expresses a need to return home the provider should refrain from passing judgment on the desirability of that decision and focus instead on helping the victim to make a plan to assure his or her safety in the event that the violence starts up again. If the victim does not feel it is safe to return home, then the provider should assist the victim to find a safe haven from further abuse. This may be the home of a friend or another more supportive family member. Victims should also be directed to sources of legal aid for assistance in obtaining a protective–restraining order or a legal guardian (in the case of an adolescent, elderly, or mentally impaired individual).

MEDICAL TREATMENT OF ADULT VICTIMS OF ABUSE

Contraception

The risk of pregnancy (Abramowicz, 1989, p. 93) following unprotected intercourse is 20 percent at three days prior to ovulation; 25 percent one day prior to ovulation; and 15 percent on the day of ovulation. The risk of becoming pregnant as a result of unprotected intercourse approaches zero two days following ovulation. High dose estrogens have been shown to significantly lower the risk of pregnancy following unprotected intercourse. However, such "postcoital contraception" is reserved for cases where the nature of the abuse could result in pregnancy (e.g., female victim of vaginal intercourse who presents for evaluation within 48 hours of the assault). In such cases, the victim should be tested for pregnancy and receive an explanation of the risks and benefits of this form of contraception prior to receiving any postcoital contraceptive drugs. The risks include the following:

1. An inability to guarantee that such treatment will prevent a pregnancy resulting from a sexual assault. The pooled failure rate is reported to be 1.8 percent (Abramowicz, 1989, p. 93).
2. Unpleasant side effects: nausea, vomiting, breast tenderness, dizziness, and menstrual irregularities.
3. Theoretical risk that the treatment may produce fetal malformations if the pregnancy continues.

A common postcoital contraceptive regimen consists of two tablets of *Ovral* (50 μg of ethinyl estradiol and 0.5 mg of norgestrel per tablet) given initially (within 72 hours of unprotected intercourse) followed 12 hours later by another two Ovral tablets (Yupze and Lancee, 1977, p. 238). Compazine 5 to 10 mg (prochlorperazine) can be given two hours prior to the second dose to prevent nausea. Other methods of postcoital contraception currently under development include progestational agents and luteinizing hormone releasing hormone analogues. *Mefepristone* (RU 486) is a competitive, progesterone antagonist which is now undergoing clinical testing in the United States.

Treatment of Sexually Transmitted Diseases

Prophylactic treatment of STDs among adult victims of sexual abuse/assault is usually provided since the incidence of STDs in this population is relatively high and the consequences of an untreated STD can be severe. Optimal antimicrobial treatment regimens for sexually transmitted diseases are published by the Centers for Disease Control (1993a).

Chart Documentation of the Medical Evaluation of Adult Abuse

The final record of the evaluation of suspected victims of abuse is an important legal document. The record should be legible and include details of the results of the history, physical exam, and the lab studies obtained during the evaluation.

Legal Issues

Legal interventions are important for adult victims of abuse (Loring and Smith, 1994, p. 335). Many adult victims (particularly battered spouses) are abused repeatedly over time before the abuse is disclosed and assistance is provided. Unfortunately, some adult victims of abuse do not always ask for protection from local police, and some states did not recognize until recently some forms of adult abuse such as "marital" rape. Moreover, the principal legal intervention: arrest of the perpetrator when the abuse is first disclosed, may not always protect the victim from subsequent abuse and may actually escalate the level of subsequent abuse. Nevertheless, physicians should encourage adult victims to report abusive incidents to police. In some instances (e.g., developmentally disabled adults, the elderly, or institutionalized adults) the victim may be unable to report abuse and the attending physician will have to make the report instead. Health care providers also have a duty to warn potential victims of domestic violence (Campbell, 1994, p. 888). This is particularly important if the provider is caring for both the abuser and the victim. In such instances the duty to warn takes precedence over the need to maintain confidentiality.

5

Domestic Violence

Lenore E. Walker, Ed.D.

We all remember the highly emotional response across the nation in the early 1990s case of Susan Smith, who drowned her two little boys. Domestic violence is one of the hottest topics in the country today, and rightfully so, because it is one of the most shameful secrets not only in our country but in countries around the world.

It is really important for us as a society, to be able to look at domestic violence and say "we want to change this." I have been working and studying in the field for the past 20 years. Interestingly, my work came from my own medical school faculty appointment back in the early 1970s, well before most people were talking about battered women. I was on the faculty of Rutgers Medical School and at first we were working with abused children. There were five women on our psychiatric faculty out of a faculty of 38 people. We were very new amongst the nation's medical schools back in 1972, but we were at the forefront in looking at the issue of child abuse. In the 1990s,

---

This paper is based on a Grand Rounds Presentation at the Department of Psychiatry, College of Medicine, University of Kentucky, 1995.

many people do not realize that in the early 1970s, very few states even had mandatory child abuse reporting laws. In those days I began to hear pejorative comments from many of the doctors that I was working with regarding the mothers who were abusing their children or who were failing to protect them from abuse. Some people say that this was when I first became a feminist—I'm not quite sure exactly when, but I know that being raised in New York City and coming of age as a woman during the 1960s when we were really dealing with issues about psychology and women, certainly contributed to my reactions in the early 1970s. At any rate, I was very concerned about all the negative comments I heard from professionals about mothers who weren't protecting their children, a situation that still exists today. I asked myself why women were being so easily blamed for failure to protect their children. Were women really very violent toward their children or were there other reasons behind it? As I began to do some of this research, it became clear to me that many mothers who failed to protect their children couldn't even protect themselves. These were the women who were being battered by the men whom they also loved and who loved them.

One of the most difficult concepts for me to understand in the early 1970s was that a person can love someone and beat someone, really hurt them at the same time. Relationships that are both loving and violent are hard to understand. Our common sense tells us that if your hurt someone, you don't love that person. But that is not true in battering relationships.

As I began to do the research, a lot of the myths that accompanied domestic violence and battering relationships became clear. For example, most of us believe ultimately, that it takes two to make a fight. Most of us were taught that if a person doesn't want to fight, that person doesn't have to fight. But in domestic violence situations, it takes one person to pick a fight and that fight will happen even if the other person, usually the woman, doesn't want to fight. She may react to the behavior in different ways, sometimes fighting back, sometimes not fighting back. Nonetheless, one person often cannot stop the fight when the other is so determined.

Common sense also tells us that if two people are telling you different versions of the same story, then the truth has to be somewhere in the middle. Again, that is not accurate when we begin to gather data about battering relationships. The truth is always worse than what either party will tell you. This is because there is so much denial and much minimization due to a horror of having to come to grips with what really is happening, and the danger of escalating violence.

Today we have a lot of research data supporting differences in the ways in which both men and women report incidents of violence. This is a field where understanding gender differences is critical. It is important to know that the data demonstrate that women are more likely to be victims and men are more likely to be perpetrators. Now, we have to account for those gender differences, but I think it's really important not to get lost in the "who hit who first; or who had more flack with whom." In the summer of 1994, there were a number of reports in the media that suggested that women hit men as often as men hit women, and therefore, they were as violent as men. And again, it depends on what study you look at and what kind of data you define as part of family violence.

I am chairing the Presidential Task Force on Violence and the Family (1996) for the American Psychological Association and we have taken a very clear, firm stand that domestic violence is not about one slap or one punch, but rather, about a pattern of behavior that includes physical, psychological, and sexual abuse, a pattern that is reinforced by the additional intimidation and fear of additional violence. If you only count a slap or punch, you miss the essence of a domestic violence relationship. When we look at the data, we have to be very clear that, yes, some studies show that women can hit as much as men. The epidemiological data show that the most frequent kind of abuse used by women is what we would call less lethal. For example, one common category named is where women "bite" men more frequently. Now, how many people know a woman who just walks up to a man and bites him? That's not the kind of violence and abuse that we're talking about. That's a defensive strategy, when someone's got the woman in some kind of arm hold.

Research studies (Walker, 1992) suggest that if you're going to count behavior or try to get incidents and preference level of behaviors you have to look at who's doing the reporting. There's a gender difference in how domestic violence acts are actually reported. Women tend to report every single kind of aggressive behavior when asked, whether or not they intended to commit that particular act. Men tend to report only incidents that were intentional, if they report them at all. So, for example, in taking data from the same couple, the woman reported, "Yes, I kicked him in the middle of the night when I was sleeping. I don't remember kicking him but he told me when we woke up that I kicked him." And she counted that as a report of her violent behavior. When we asked the man, "Were you kicked?" he said, "No. She didn't kick me." Later we went back to him and said, "But wait a second, your wife said she kicked you in the middle of the night and you told her that she did," and he said, "Forget that, it doesn't count. She didn't mean to kick me. She was sleeping." So, he like many men, was less likely to report nonintentional acts than are women. Now that suggests that there will then be a bias toward more reporting for women than for men, which may account for some of the data that says that within hitting and slapping, and biting and kicking behaviors, women may be equal to men in some situations.

Why do we make a fuss about all of the physical and psychological and sexual abuse? Why should we as health service professionals get involved in wanting to know about domestic violence? Well, for one reason, we know that being exposed to repeated abuse has psychological effects for many victims. We don't know how many victims of domestic violence we actually have in any country or any society. If you take the data based upon the number of cases that are reported to the U.S. Justice Department, you get a number of approximately 2.5 million women each year being physically abused. We don't have a clue as to how many of those women or other women are sexually abused since those data, unlike physical violence, are not recorded. If you add in the data from civil restraining orders, not just criminal assaults, then your data grows to about 3 to 4 million. And if you start estimating all of the women who never report to anyone, the numbers become astronomical.

When I first started doing this research, I suggested that the numbers may be as high as one out of two women. Today, the numbers range from one out of four to one out of three women, will be abused at some point over a lifetime, not just a one-year period, as the other numbers project. So, we're talking about a large number of women but only a small number of men. The criminal and the Justice Department reports show 95 out of every 100 victims of "spouse abuse" are women. Five out of those 100 cases are men who are abused. So men are also battered in relationships, but not at anywhere near the same frequency as women. Again, we can look at the gender issue. The research data shows that violence passes from one generation to another. Now, these data are very difficult and very complex from which to make predictions. About the best data that we have again, are Straus and Gelles (1990) epidemiological data. They suggested that a little boy who witnessed his father batter his mother was 700 times more likely than a child who did not experience this violence to be abusive to others during his life. Seven hundred more times the risk factor! If that little boy was not just exposed to violence in his home, but also abused, it raised that risk factor to one thousand times the norm. Those are huge statistics when you look at risk factors. That suggests that we really have to do something about males and females in our society and the kind of messages that they are getting in these violent homes. We can't talk about predictions; we can't support the statement that a little boy who watches his father batter his mother is going to grow up to be a batterer with any great predictive numbers because we just don't know. Obviously, there are children who are exposed to domestic violence who don't grow up and hurt anyone. That's the population we have not studied yet, and it is an area that should be studied because that data we really need.

What about the people who are battered just one time? What happens to them? Or the perpetrators who use violence just once and stop? What makes them just stop using violence? We have no idea. We know something about their victims. We know more about batterers today because we have the courts helping us get batterers into treatment programs. We now know that batterers probably span at least three different topologies. We no longer talk about *a* batterer, we talk about the different kinds of batterers.

The research suggests that there are three batterer topologies. The first group includes men who are violent only in their families, and not just to women but other family members as well. These men are using violence as a means of power and control. The second group includes men who have diagnosable mental illnesses. They may also be like part of that first group who use violence for power and control. But there's also some significant mental illness that goes along with the violence. They are often schizophrenics, paranoid, and sometimes suffer from depression. Sometimes we'll see some personality disorders, but these men are different from those who use violence as a means of entitlement to get what they want from the woman. And, then there is a third group, who are antisocial. These men also commit other crimes in addition to using violence in their homes. Most of those in this particular group do not respond to our treatment plans because we simply don't know how to help them stop their violence. The literature suggests that the largest group may be the first one I mentioned, the men who use violence as a means of power and control and a sense of entitlement in their own homes; the other two groups are smaller. But in fact, the research is just beginning in that area and we simply don't have good data.

We know that many batterers do stop their violence, their physical abuse, and many of our treatment programs, particularly the longer-term programs that are offender-specific, that deal specifically with the offense and stopping the violence, are successful at stopping the physical violence for at least some period of time. The longest follow-up study that I have seen is about 18 months in length, although I think there may be one or two two-year follow-up studies. We really don't have good data and knowledge whether the treatment and intervention programs stop all forms of violence, particularly psychological and sexual abuse, over a long period of time. We also have some data to suggest that some batterers, and we believe that they are the batterers in the first group (needing power, control, and entitlement) are able to stop their violence on arrest. Usually arrest, being held in jail, usually overnight, is sufficient for some men to stop their physical abuse. But others may become so enraged that they increase their violence following an arrest. So, we must be careful when making recommendations.

Now, stopping psychological abuse is another question and there's much less data that suggests we are successful in stopping psychological torture and intimidation.

So, we have been doing a lot since the early 1970s when I first got involved in domestic violence. Most of the battering research is from the mid- to late-1980s. It is during these last few years that we see some important new research studies about perpetrators. I use the euphemism *domestic violence* to mean battered women and adult abuse. The term *family violence* is usually used to encompass child abuse, as well as adult abuse. But we know in many families the abuse doesn't stop with the woman, it also includes the children. And we know that children who are exposed to violence are at high risk to develop all kinds of psychological and behavioral problems in addition to becoming violent themselves. Many of the problems look very similar to the other kinds of difficulties experienced by children who were exposed to other kinds of child maltreatment. So our work with child abuse has to be expanded to include those children who are at risk because of exposure to violence in the home.

THERAPY WITH BATTERED WOMEN

The earliest therapy attempted with battered women was unsuccessful. There were reports when I did my research in the late 1970s and early 1980s, from interviews with 400 battered women, many of whom told us that they had been in family or group psychotherapy, sometimes many years of individual psychotherapy, and never told their therapists that they were abused. Or if they told their therapists about the abuse, the therapists gave the message that it was inconsequential and so the women didn't talk about it anymore. It was simply not an issue to be raised. Occasionally, there were therapists who suggested that the victims were masochistic. The whole issue of a masochistic personality disorder came up again in the mid-1980s and psychiatrists talked about putting such a diagnostic category back into the DSM-III-R (APA, 1987). Eventually, it was included, but it was renamed Self-Defeating Personality Disorder—it has been taken out of DSM-IV. Most battered women who demonstrate symptoms of Battered Woman Syndrome and need a diagnostic label, receive a diagnosis of posttraumatic stress disorder (PTSD).

The PTSD category helps mental health professionals better deal with the issues; the description and understanding of what happens to a woman when she is exposed to violence. Now, I can say clinically from my own work that the patterns are similar but we simply don't have enough evidence to say that this is really a *battered woman syndrome* (BWS) *or battered person syndrome,* terms that the courts like to use. It is easy to be fair and say BWS should be gender neutral, but that isn't true. The research data available are about women; so we have to be clear that what we're talking about is Battered *Woman* Syndrome. Battered Woman Syndrome symptoms are very similar to PTSD, but not identical. What appears to be different is the extent to which symptoms of Battered Woman's Syndrome must be internalized because of the threat of physical harm. Think about what happens to someone when they are exposed to repeated trauma, particularly in situations where the trauma is administered by the very person who is also nice to them or who loves them. It is a fight or flight response based on dissonant experience.

One way to take care of and protect oneself if exposed to trauma is to become alert and physiologically ready so that you can deal with that trauma. That is the high anxiety response that we see as part of BWS syndrome, usually more pervasive than other symptoms of PTSD. On the other hand, most people, being afraid of trauma, want to get away from a traumatic situation as quickly and as calmly as they can. But if you can't physically get out, then you can psychologically get out. And that's what we talk about when we use the terms *denial, repression,* and *dissociation,* which are methods of getting our minds out of harm's way (the perpetrator's way) and then, the emotional numbing violence and depression.

Exposure to trauma changes how we think about things, and impacts our memories, although this is a controversial subject today. Some victims keep forgetting, or remember abuse in a different way from memories of other types of things. So, those three areas (1) high arousal and anxiety, (2) high avoidance and numbing, and (3) cognitive and memory changes are the major areas of BWS, a subcategory of PTSD. Now, with BWS, you also have some effects in additional areas, including the shaping of interpersonal relationships that are very tenuous. Women become more isolated and they become less trusting of other people, and if you're not with them, on their side, you will not be trusted. In fact, objectivity about relationships is simply gone. It means you are against them, and health professionals will see that reaction from many clients. If you are not with them, then to be a good clinician means to be a different kind of therapist from the neutral objective therapist that many people learn to be. I certainly learned how to stay neutral when I was being trained. But for a battered woman, a health care person who is being objective and neutral is perceived as being ''against'' them. There has to be some demonstration of understanding and validation of the client's problems, including abuse issues. And I call this new therapy, ''survivor therapy,'' which is a blending of standard feminist therapy principles and trauma therapy principles. In feminist therapy, we are very careful about our impact in the therapy relationship. We learn to monitor ourselves. We learn to give our client explicit help, so that the client can be able to become what we call ''empowered.'' We empower her to assume some control of her life. We encourage that. And, in addition, in trying to be very clear about negotiating the goals of treatment, but without advocating our goals for the client, we help her make such decisions without giving advice. And that's not an easy role to take on for many therapists, but it's an important one when we deal with battered women. And if we don't do that, we won't know how reliable or valid our information is. We also must remember to strengthen, validate, and empower the woman.

To help the client go from being a victim to becoming a survivor, two goals are essential. First, we must help her become safe and, second, we must help her establish her own sense of personal power. An essential tenet of this treatment approach is for the therapist to take care not to blame the victim for being abused.

6

Adult Nonsurvivors of Abusive Relationships

The long-term effects of victimization in childhood have a significant impact on adaptation in adulthood. The characteristics of individuals who are adult survivors and nonsurvivors of child abuse are examined, and a case study is presented of an individual who was abused as a child and now experiences nonsurvivor adulthood. A dysfunctional childhood has resulted in considerable failure in coping with and adjusting to adult stresses and has resulted in the development of psychopathology that has impaired adaptation to adult life. Issues and import for clinical practice and future research are explored.

SURVIVORS AND NONSURVIVORS

Some survivors of traumatic and stressful life experiences have experienced abuse, and neglect as children, and sexual abuse (Green, Wilson, and Lindy, 1985; Browne and Finkelhor, 1986; Rieker and Carmen, 1986; Jacobson, Koehler, and Jones-Brown, 1987; Gise and Paddison,

1988; Walker, 1994). In assessing the adaptation of victims of child abuse and child sexual abuse, the ability of the individual to cope effectively and to experience a social support system is of critical importance (Schatzow and Herman, 1989; Biden, 1993). Inadequate social support or a lack of adequate coping skills make the likelihood of adjustment difficulties in adulthood much more likely.

It is the adult nonsurvivor (Miller and Veltkamp, 1989b) who can show such clinical symptoms as low self-esteem, self-hatred, poor control of aggression, unstable affect, and dysfunctional relationships (Rieker and Carmen, 1986). In addition, these researchers found comorbidity in this sample, including borderline personality disorder and anorexia nervosa. Conte, Berliner, and Schuerman (1987) suggest that as many as 20 percent of all adults who were sexually abused as children show serious psychopathology in adulthood and show a likely comorbidity with the DSM-IV diagnosis of posttraumatic stress disorder (PTSD).

One study (*Harvard Mental Health Letter,* 1993) found that symptoms of PTSD occurred in 44 percent of sexually abused children including 54 percent of those abused by fathers and 10 percent of those abused by strangers. Symptoms experienced as children can also be seen in victims during their adulthood. In addition, under the stress of severe physical or sexual abuse, victims may try to defend themselves by imagining that they are elsewhere, and dissociating from experiencing the trauma.

The rage of victims may be turned against themselves, the world in general, or specific people, particularly the nonoffending spouse or anyone else who failed to protect them. A woman who was abused as a girl may allow herself to be further abused by men both physically and sexually, accepting degradation as a price of any intimate relationship. On the other hand, males are less likely to admit their feeling about having been sexually or physically abused and may see themselves as bad rather than accept the status of victim. By turning their rage outward and attacking others, they make themselves feel powerful instead of helpless. Sexually abused males are often confused about their sexual identity. The *Harvard Mental Health Letter* reports that at least 20 to 40 percent of people with borderline personalities have no memory of childhood abuse and show no signs of it.

A heavy atmosphere of secrecy and denial still surrounds child sexual abuse, both as a family problem and social issue. Most of it never comes to light (Blume, 1990). Probably fewer than 10 percent of the cases are reported to the police or child protective services.

The adult nonsurvivor of child abuse is defined as a person who, as a result of this victimization, experiences a massive failure in his or her adult life, as well as in the ability to cope with life stresses. The resulting psychopathology often finds them in conflict with psychosocial and legal systems in our society (Braver, Blumberg, Green, Rawson, 1992).

Patterns of Abuse and Accommodation

Abuse has been the focus of several research studies (Veltkamp, Miller, Kearl, Barlow-Elliot, and Bright, 1992; Gomez-Schwartz, Horowitz, and Sauzier, 1985; Finkelhor, 1984). Summit (1983) developed the Sexual Abuse Accommodation Syndrome. This model suggests that victims who are sexually abused are often fearful and confused about the outcome of disclosure in sexual abuse situations. Health care professionals and court officials may offer little support and sometime disbelieve the child in this process. This leads Summit to suggest five phases of the syndrome, which include secrecy, helplessness, accommodation, delayed disclosure, and retraction (see Figure 6.1) all of which have wide application to all victims of abuse.

Perpetrators may be recognized by certain psychological risk factors, which include but are not limited to the following:

- Isolation from other individuals
- Poor self-esteem
- Difficulty expressing anger
- Highly impulsive
- High ratio of negative to positive interactions
- High rates of actual and perceived stress
- May use sex as an act of aggression

Likewise, the accommodation of this traumatic experience suggests the likely presence of a Trauma Accommodation Syndrome realized

Figure 6.1 Sexual Abuse Accommodation Syndrome (Summit, 1983)

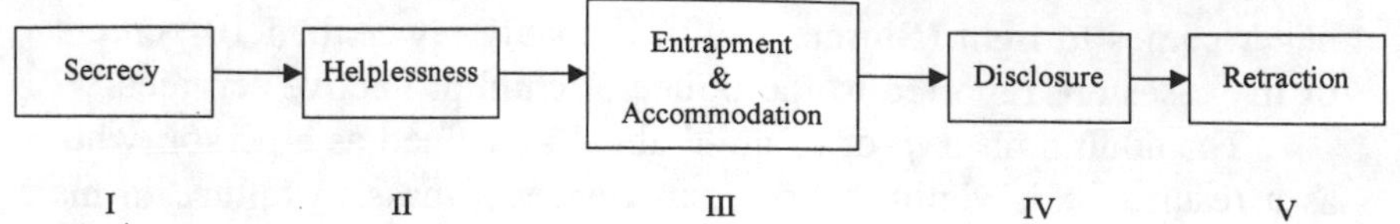

by the sexual victimization. Veltkamp and Miller (1994) suggest that the victimized person moves through a series of stages, or phases, as summarized in Figure 6.2.

THE IMPACT OF CHRONIC AND PERVASIVE CHILD ABUSE IN ADULTHOOD CASE STUDY

A 23-year-old single white female is the product of a multigenerational family of child and adult abusers. As a child, she was victimized on a number of occasions. The patient's history reveals that her early childhood years were chaotic and unpredictable. Her parents separated when she was approximately 4, and their relationship was characterized by considerable marital discord and father's abuse of drugs and alcohol, and violent abuse of mother, much of which was observed by the patient. During these early years, she lived in five foster homes, as well as living with her mother and maternal grandmother, moving approximately 15 times. During the first seven years of her life, she was subjected to sexual abuse by a great-uncle, physical abuse, and the psychological trauma that occurs when a parent is repeatedly abused verbally and physically battered.

The impact of these early life experiences took a substantial toll on her ability to trust, led to the development of a negative self-image, and a reservoir of anger and rage, which at times was expressed outwardly, and at other times toward herself. A sense of learned helplessness during these early years developed in terms of her ability (1) to take care of herself; (2) to ask for help; and (3) to develop relationships. Prior to adolescence, the patient's life continued to be chaotic and unpredictable. Her attempts to get the attention of her parents were often met with rejection or abandonment. By age 11, she

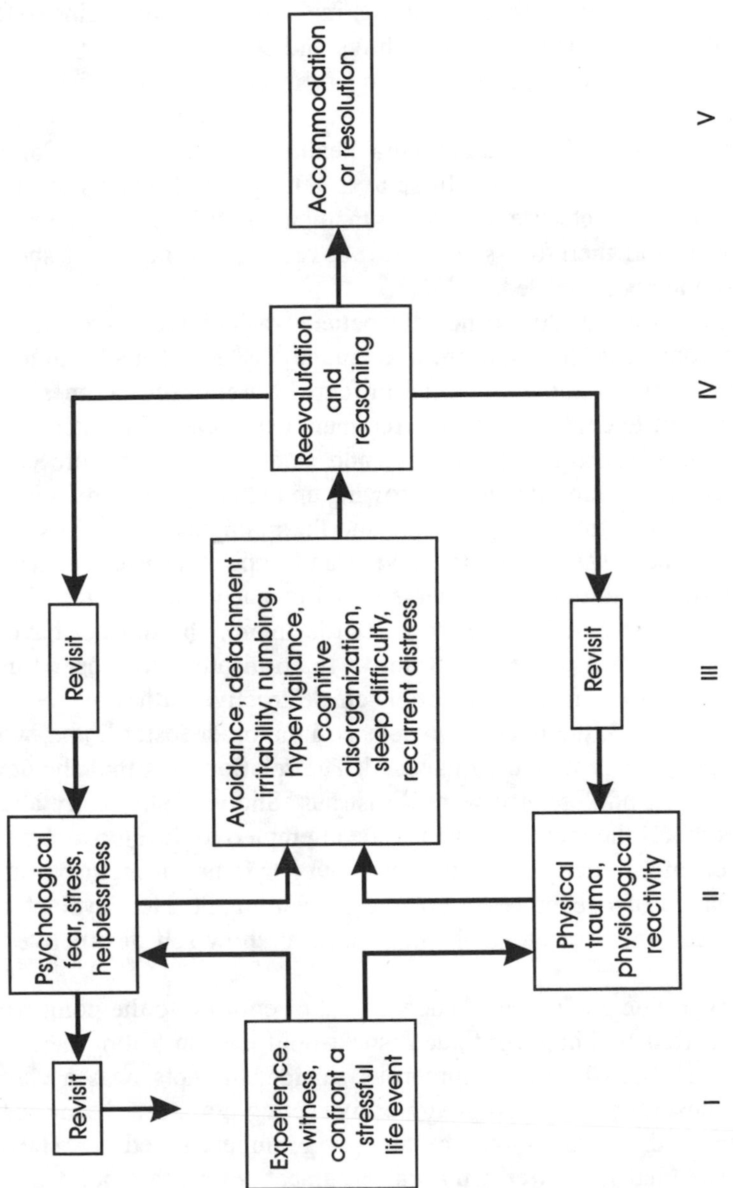

Figure 6.2 Trauma Accommodation Syndrome

had made her first suicide attempt, an apparent effort to get her mother's attention, whom she felt was rejecting her in favor of her stepfather. During ages 12 through 15, there are frequent instances of truancy, fights, and substance abuse, including glue and paint sniffing and other experimentation with drugs and sex.

The patient changed schools on 6 different occasions during grade school, averaging two changes per year. On more than one occasion, she saw both physicians and mental health professionals at a Community Mental Health Center. In spite of telling the clinicians about her abuse, there is clear evidence from their records that she was not believed, and therefore she could not receive the help that she and family members needed.

During early adolescence, the patient was involved in regular drug and alcohol use, prostitution, and truancy. She had made numerous suicide attempts and was placed in four different group homes which provided little continuity in her treatment experience. The alcohol and drug abuse, prostitution, truancy, and suicide attempts were coping mechanisms she learned while growing up in her dysfunctional family. Running away from the problems and the manipulation and exploitation of others was a way to survive and cope. She learned that she could turn to no one except herself, and by early adolescence, she did not have trust or faith in anyone. Furthermore, she did not have the ability to form positive, constructive relationships, no longer trusted the helping system, and was on a self-destructive path.

By age 15, the patient was placed in another foster home, where she was again exploited and abused. The relationships that she developed during adolescence were disastrous. She was physically abused by nearly all the men with whom she attempted to develop a romantic relationship. Every attempt to search out her father or mother resulted in feelings of deeper rejection and abandonment. Her level of rage and anger only escalated; she continued to show self-destructive tendencies.

With late adolescence, she was out of control, to the point where she felt that if things continued, she would end up killing herself or someone else. She made numerous suicide attempts, was a chronic drug abuser, and engaged in aggressive acting out. After living for six months with a man whom she thought geniunely loved her, she shot and wounded him after a marital argument. From this point on, the

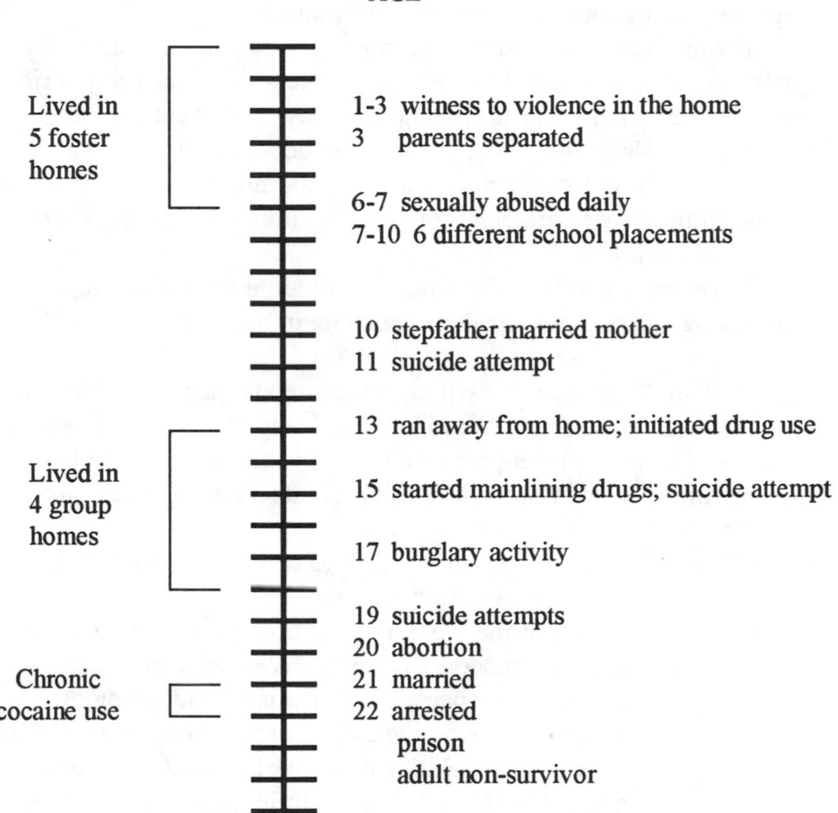

Figure 6.3 Lifeline chart of dysfunctional behaviors contributing to "nonsurvivor" status

patient's life became totally disorganized. She immersed herself in drugs, particularly cocaine. She no longer had the will to live, using drugs only as measure of surviving for another day.

Having been arrested for cocaine possession and after three months in jail, she returned to the streets, and during a nine-day period, used cocaine heavily, up to 15 grams a day, and went the last four days without sleep, suffering from sleep deprivation. She was at a point where her self-destructive pattern could not continue and could only be stopped by suicide, or violent acting out, or being apprehended by the authorities.

There are a number of themes that emerge which are important in assessing the psychological components in this case:

- The multigenerational pattern of abuse and neglect, which goes back at least four generations and leads to a sense of learned helplessness on the part of all family members, particularly in dealing with conflict, relationships, and feelings of anger and depression.
- There is a long history of severe and continued family dysfunction, including inadequate parenting.
- The seriousness of the patient's psychological problems, going back into her childhood, are extreme. Even prior to adolescence, she was abusing substances, being a truant, and acting out in a violent manner. This was indicative of the rage, distortion of perceptions regarding relationships, caring, and love, and the inability to attach or bond. There is little question that she suffered from attachment disorders.
- There is a lifelong pattern of self-destructive patterns of behavior, which include suicide, beating herself, chronic substance abuse, truancy, and involvement with abusive men, etc.
- There is a repeated failure on the part of various agencies and professionals to properly identify, evaluate, and treat the patient's problems. In addition, there is evidence that she was placed, at least twice, in homes where she was sexually abused.
- The lack of stability and security throughout the patient's life is obvious. As a preteen, she lived in several foster homes. She had changed schools several times during her elementary school years. In adolescence, she was in four group homes.

ERRORS IN PROFESSIONAL JUDGMENT

The evaluation revealed that during the patient's life, particularly her childhood, records indicate numerous errors in professional judgment:

1. During the first seven years she was moved approximately 15 times.
2. She was repeatedly returned to her parents in spite of the well-known history of substance abuse, spousal abuse, and neglect of the children.
3. At age 7 she was placed in a foster home where she was sexually abused.
4. Two mental health professionals did not believe patient's detailed and vivid account of her sexual victimization at age 7.
5. From ages 6 to 12, she was moved to 12 different classrooms in 6 different schools, an average of two per year.
6. Family therapy was repeatedly recommended in spite of the established fact that this dysfunctional family was beyond rehabilitation.
7. During adolescence, she was placed in four group homes, all of them different, failing to provide continuity of treatment.
8. At age 15, she was placed in a home with a 63-year old male attendant who sexually misused and abused her.
9. Failure to terminate parental rights.

Mental health, health, and legal professionals must take their decision making seriously.

DISCUSSION

Miller and Veltkamp (1993) and Walker (1994) indicate that those individuals significantly abused in childhood may show the identified pattern of "adult nonsurvivors" in adulthood. The clinical profile of the adult nonsurvivor of child abuse recognizes a multigenerational pattern of abuse. It identifies as well a predictable pattern of decompensation if treatment does not take place. The profile addresses characteristics which are often seen in abusive families.

Gold (1986) explored the relation between childhood victimization experience and adult functioning. One hundred and three adult women who were victimized as children or adolescents served as subjects, and 88 women who were not victimized served as controls. Members of both groups completed a questionnaire about their present social, psychological, and sexual functioning. Sexually victimized women also provided information about their victimization experiences. Victimized women differed significantly from nonvictims on measures of: (1) childhood family and social experiences; (2) adult attributional style; and (3) level of depression, psychological distress, self-esteem, and sexual problems.

Results of this study suggested that the sexually victimized women's adult functioning was related most strongly to their attributional style for negative events. Perception of the victimization experience and quality of social support were also important factors related to adult functioning.

While Briere (1984) suggests that as many as one of every four girls in North America may be sexually victimized before she reaches adulthood, recent studies show that not close to half of all women who have received help in clinical settings were sexually victimized as children. While most studies have found that some victims exhibit no specific pattern of response to childhood sexual abuse, certain symptoms of posttraumatic stress are commonly observed. These include depression, low self-esteem, guilt feelings, and interpersonal difficulties characterized by feelings of isolation and difficulty in trusting others. Symptoms such as these are clearly evident in the case summarized.

Finkelhor (1984) points out that the following symptoms, all indicators of nonsurvivorship, are seen in adults who were sexually victimized as children: (1) inappropriate sexualization of parenting; (2) drug and alcohol abuse; (3) criminal involvement; (4) self-mutilization; (5) suicide; (6) vulnerability to subsequent abuse.

In summary, the long-term effects of child abuse in adulthood reveal the following:

1. There is clear evidence of self-destructive behaviors in victimized from nonvictimized patients. In the case study self-destructive behaviors emerged in childhood and continued into adulthood. These are seen both in suicidal and homicidal activities.

2. Women who have been abused show significant adjustment difficulties in problems related to both interpersonal and sexual relationships with males and females as adults. More specifically, it appears that incest victims carry hostile feelings toward significant adults in their adulthood. In the case cited, the homicidal activity is a clear indication of these intense feelings.
3. Sexually abused female children may as adults seek relationships which involve sexual or physical abuse. Herein, the case reveals that two of three male partners were physically abusive to the adult nonsurvivor, and in the case of the husband who was not abusive, a violent response was realized when the patient shot him.
4. The most significant diagnostic profile for adults who are physically and sexually abused as children includes the following symptomatology: Depression, self-destructive behavior, anxiety, traumatic stress, feelings of isolation, poor self-esteem, a tendency toward revictimization, substance abuse, difficulties in trusting others, and sexual maladjustment in adulthood.

It is clear from the research in the Harvard Maltreatment Project (Cicchetti and Olsen, 1987) that most maltreated individuals have experienced more than one distinct type of maltreatment; that siblings of maltreated individuals are highly likely to be maltreated; even though their maltreatment experience may not be legally documented; that different types of maltreatment have differential impact on various domains of development; and that many maltreated individuals have insecure attachment relationships with their caregivers and guardians.

With respect to nonsurvivor perpetrators of abuse, there appears to be several psychological risk factors including: isolation from family, friends, and others; expressed anger toward self and others; poor impulsivity and control; affective inability; inappropriate expectations of the victim; high ratio of negative to positive interactions; high rates of actual and perceived stress.

7

The Perpetrator: Personality Parameters of Abuse

INTRODUCTION

Clinicians and researchers have searched for personality characteristics related to the psychopathology of the perpetrator. If perpetrators could be identified in advance, efforts to intervene or prevent abuse would be substantially enhanced. The relationship between victim and perpetrator is generally differentiated by issues related to power and control. Efforts to use various psychological measures to assess the presence of psychopathology in perpetrators of abuse have met with limited success (Dadds, Smith, and Webber, 1991). In this study, MMPI profiles failed to detect any level of psychopathology in nonincarcerated perpetrators of abuse. Likewise, Taylor, Murphy, Jellink, Quinn, Poitrast, and Goshko (1991) in examination of parents who acted abusively toward their children, found consistently in the clinical literature that abusing parents seldom displayed psychotic tendencies. Burgess, Hazelwood, Rokous, and Hartman (1993) found that early sexual abuse is often followed by reenactment behavior. Summarized in Table 7.1

are risk factors and clinical indicators for potential perpetrators of abuse.

Finkelhor (1984) argues that dissociation may be very significant in denial of abuse or in denial of the harm it can cause to its victim. Psychoactive substance abuse may be implicated at least 50 percent of the time in various categories of abuse. The disinhibition which accompanies the abuse of alcohol and drugs permits a host of impulses to come to the fore which are involved in various types of perpetration, accompanied by lack of control, and thus disinhibition. The psychopathological conditions most frequently seen in perpetrators are seen in character disorders or what have come to be known in DSM-IV criteria as personality disorders. There are several risk factors that emerge in identifying perpetrators. These include the need for power and control; high levels of actual and perceived stress; difficulty in expressing anger; impulsivity; high incidence of negative interactions with various family members; isolated life-styles; emotional immaturity; having been abused or neglected; having been exposed to parental violence; and poor self-esteem.

MEN WHO ABUSE WOMEN

Walker (1979, 1994) discusses the common characteristics of men who abuse and batter. Variability in all demographics is noted. In the population she studied, the youngest batterer was described as 16 years of age and the oldest was 76. It is significant that they are generally unrecognizable to the uniformed observer and not distinguished by demographic data. The typical individual who is a batterer presents the following profile:

- Poor self-esteem.
- Blames others for his actions.
- Tends to be pathologically jealous.
- May present a dual personality.
- Believes the myths about battering relationships.
- Tends to be a traditionalist, believing in male supremacy.
- Often has stereotypical masculine sex-role identity.

Table 7.1 Risk Factors and Clinical Indicators for Potential Violent Abusers

Clinical Indicators	Low	Medium	High
Family Life	Wanted child, good loving family	Occasional family disruption, loss of a parent or one-parent family	Early violence, battered child, poor parental model
Significant Others	Several reliable family members or friends available	Few or one available	None available
Daily Functioning	Good in most activities	Moderately good in some activities	Not good in any activities
Life-Style	Stable	Moderately stable	Unstable
Employment	Employed	Employment history fairly stable	Unemployed
Education	High-school graduate or more (university or technical training)	High-school dropout, can read and write	School dropout, to illiterate
Living Conditions	Lives in adequate housing, clean environment and space	Fair housing, some overcrowding	Poor housing, crowded, slums
Isolation or Withdrawal	Able to relate well to others, outgoing	Mild, some withdrawal and feelings of hopelessness	Long history of being a loner, antisocial, withdrawn, hopeless, helpless feelings
Alcohol or Drug Abuse	Nondrinker, or occasional social use	Social drinker or user to occasional abuse	Chronic abuse
Psychological History	No history of need for or use of psychiatric hospitalization	Some outpatient psychiatric help, moderately satisfied with self	History of psychiatric hospitalization, negative view of help
Personal History	No history of violence or impulsive behavior	Occasional history of violence or impulsive behavior	Frequent history of violence or impulsive behavior

- Has severe stress reactions.
- Uses alcohol and drugs and wife battering as a medium to cope with stress.
- Frequently uses sex as an act of aggression.
- Tends to enhance self-esteem at the expense of others.
- Fails to realize his violent behavior has negative consequences for others.

PARENTS AS PERPETRATORS

Goodyear (1990) studied infants and maternal depression and found depression to be clinically significant in perpetrators. In Taylor et al. (1991), one-fourth of the abusive parents were found to have severe depression. Depressed mothers were also found to criticize their children more and tested lower for affective expression. Whipple and Webster-Stratton (1991) examined parental stress in abusive families. Results suggest that parental depression was shown to be associated with harshness of discipline and decreased effectiveness in handling discipline problems.

Parents who murder their children have been more widely discussed. Examples include Susan Smith, who admitted sending her car to the bottom of a lake with her two young children strapped inside. Elizabeth Diane Downs, an Oregon mail carrier, claimed a shaggy-haired stranger waved down her car on a deserted road in 1983 and shot her three children, killing one of them and injuring the other two. She was convicted of shooting the children and herself in 1984. She claimed her father molested her when she was a child. She was later diagnosed with a host of personality disorders, and still maintains her original story about the assault. Murder statistics among parents who kill reveal the disturbing prevalence of child murder in our society. Approximately 16 percent of murder victims are members of the perpetrator's family, and parents were the murderers in 57 percent of cases involving children under the age of 12. Among parents who murder their children, there appears to be a mix of dissociation, attachment disorder, and denial. It is not uncommon to find, as in the case of both Susan Smith and Elizabeth Diane Downs, that there is a history of sexual victimization or physical abuse. The presence of physical abuse or sexual victimization can contribute to impulsivity on the part of the parent to abuse and murder their own child. In the case of Susan Smith, her father killed himself when she was 7, and she had reportedly been sexually abused by her stepfather and attempted suicide herself.

Among parents who kill, there may be a form of Munchausen syndrome by proxy, wherein parents secretly make their children ill to satisfy their own craving for attention and nurturing. In these causes, the parents may kill their children to get attention from a lover or others. The following characteristics may be seen in individuals who present with this type of disorder:

- Vagueness and inconsistency
- Pathological lying
- Denial
- Dissociation, history of abuse
- Desire for attention and nurturance

Parental perpetrators were also found to assess their children's behavior more negatively than independent raters when comparing them to a control group of parents assessing their own children. Finally, Zuravin (1989), also in a study of depressed maternal perpetrators, found that child-abusing behavior and physical and verbal aggression were state dependent in these mothers, occurring only when they are depressed. Depressed mothers were found to be at risk for higher levels of physical and verbal aggression against their children, significantly more than were control groups.

In addition, Lenore Walker (1994) reports that mothers who are abused in their marital relationships are eight times more likely to abuse their children.

SIBLING, CHILD, OR ADOLESCENT PERPETRATOR

In considering commonalities among sibling, child, or adolescent perpetrators, several psychological risk factors emerge in individuals who are abusive. These include:

- Isolation from family and friends
- High level of expressed anger and impulsivity
- High ratio of negative to positive interactions with family members
- Inappropriate expectations of others
- Strong need for power and control
- High rates of actual and perceived stress in the perpetrator's life
- Low self-esteem, feelings of worthlessness
- Having been exposed to violence in their family

O'Brien and Bera (1986) have identified different types of adolescent sexual offenders.

- The naive experimenter is usually age 11 to 14 with little previous history of acting out, engages in single or a few isolated events with children ages 2 through 6. They commonly use no force or threats and the primary motivation for abuse is to explore and experiment.
- The undersocialized child exploiter usually has few friends, gravitates toward children who admire or accept him, is internally dominated by feelings of inadequacy and insecurity, and shows little history of acting out. Family history includes an overinvolved mother and distant father. Abusive behavior involves a chronic pattern of sexual behaviors with children that include the use of manipulation, trickery, enticement, and rewards. The motivation is an attempt to achieve intimacy, a sense of importance and autonomy.
- The pseudosocialized childhood exploiter is usually an older adolescent with fairly good social skills, comfortable with peers, may be a victim of early childhood abuse, and is likely a parentfied child. Their abusive behavior often lasts for some years with little remorse or guilt. He or she characterizes the abuse as mutual and noncoercive. The motivation is the guiltless and narcissistic exploitation of a vulnerable child to gain sexual pleasure.
- The sexual aggressor is typically a product of a disorganized and abusive family, has good social skills, a long history of

antisocial behavior, poor impulse control, and fighting with family members; there is frequent abuse of chemicals. Psychological testing usually reveals an antisocial personality-disordered person.

- The sexual compulsive comes from a rigidly enmeshed family which is emotionally repressed. He or she engages in repetitive sexually arousing behavior, such as window peeping, obscene phone calls, exhibitionism.
- The disturbed impulsive has a history of abusive family relationships and substance abuse. The sexual abuse is characterized by impulsive behavior, reflecting an acute disturbance of reality testing. The offense may reflect a malfunction of normal inhibitory mechanisms due to thought disturbance or disorder or chemical abuse.
- Group influenced abusers are usually younger teens who are not likely to have past contact with the juvenile justice system. The sex abuse occurs with a peer group present, and the victim tends to be known by the offenders. The motivation for the sexually abusive behavior can be the result of peer pressure or expectations or attempts to gain acceptance and may be realized through gang rape.

Walker (1994) discusses the generational cycle of violence, which aids in our understanding of sibling, child, and adolescent perpetrators. In the generational cycle of violence, children learn and accept violence as siblings and adolescents, as well as adults. They become abusive to others including their own children. The generational cycle of violence is summarized in Figure 7.1.

Katz (1981) studied male adolescent child molesters and found these individuals statistically to be significantly more depressed than nonmolesters. Becker, Kaplan, Tenke, and Tartaglini (1991) also, in a study of depression in child molesters, found adolescent child molesters to have a poor self-image and to often repress their feelings of depression. Johnson (Johnson, Hashprodie, and Lindsay, 1993), in assessing molesters of female adolescents, found most were victims themselves and found that statistically in all cases, there were significantly higher levels of depression. Also present with respect to psychopathology were elevated feelings of anger, confusion, and anxiety. In

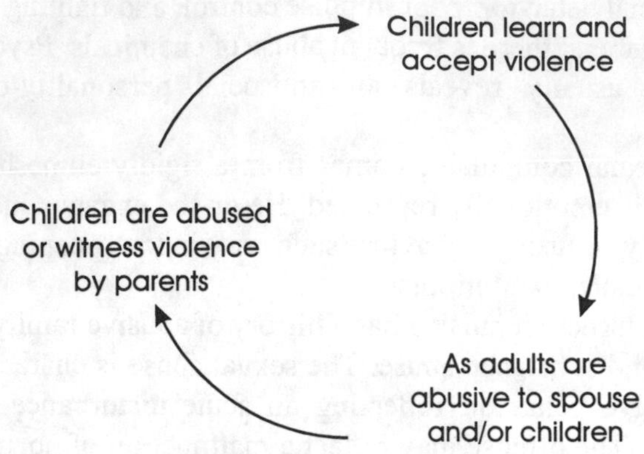

Figure 7.1 The Generational Cycle of Violence

this study, all acknowledged the wrongfulness of their behavior, but seemed oblivious to the effect that it had on their victims, which suggests a lack of empathy and understanding and also supports the multigenerational perspective of perpetration from former victims of abuse.

Approximately 300 cases of children who kill their parents are reported annually, representing less than 1 percent of all homicides each year. These children have a number of important characteristics, including the fact that they often discuss the murder in advance, usually among peers, come from dysfunctional families, and have parents who generally are extremely rigid. Risk factors for parricide often include but are not limited to:

1. Dysfunctional family
2. Emotional immaturity
3. Social isolation
4. Desire for peer approval or acceptance
5. Having been abused as a child
6. Having been exposed to parental violence
7. Feelings of worthlessness
8. Use of alcohol
9. Substance abuse
10. Adjustment difficulties in home, school, and among peers

The adult child of an elderly individual can become a perpetrator, often in the course of acting as a caregiver. This abusive behavior can include a variety of factors, including:

1. Psychological maltreatment
2. Humiliation
3. Confinement
4. Withholding of food
5. Denial of emotional responsiveness
6. Neglect of physical health
7. Neglect of mental health

The pattern of interactions that make up psychological abuse includes behaviors that range from humiliation to scapegoating, isolation, screaming, and rage. Often the extremes of this include psychological inaccessibility and rejection on the part of the caregiver. Included as a psychological maltreatment is neglect, in which the caregiver's responsibility to another human being either deliberately or by extraordinarily inattention permits the victim to experience avoidable suffering or fails to provide one or more of the ingredients generally deemed essential for the person's physical, intellectual, and emotional well-being. Neglect can occur also when a caregiver fails to provide for the needs of the individual, not out of malice or inattentiveness but simply by failing to provide for the health care of the individual being neglected, regardless of cause or rationale.

WOMEN WHO KILL MEN

The incidence of male batterers being killed by the women they abuse has increased markedly in recent years. Some states report a 25 percent increase in such cases. According to Lenore Walker (1996), women who kill can be set apart from women who do not kill by the following characteristics:

- Their perception of the dangerousness of the situation.
- The more danger the women perceive in their current relationship, the more likely they are to strike back.

- Increased alcohol abuse by the batterer.
- Sexual violence toward and rape of the women.
- Physical and sexual abuse of their children.

In fact the sexual abuse of the children was frequently viewed as the "last straw" leading to the murder. Lenore Walker believes that the behavior of women who kill should be viewed as a response to an unresponsive system. "Defending oneself from perceived imminent danger of bodily harm or death should be considered a healthy response, not an unhealthy response" (1994, p. 168).

PERPETRATOR PERSONALITY PROFILE

Recent studies associated with perpetrators reveal the following characteristics (Katz, 1990; Heap, 1991; Taylor et al., 1991):

- Poor social skills
- Inadequate expression of feelings
- Poor impulse control
- Lack of empathy
- Unstable patterns of interpersonal behavior
- Affective inability
- Inappropriate and intense anger

In addition, diagnostic features may include the following:

- Failure to conform to social norms
- Poor impulse control
- Identity and role diffusion
- Pattern of unstable interpersonal relationships
- Affective instability
- Inability to control anger
- Transient paranoid ideation
- Real or imagined abandonment
- Self-mutilating behavior

Pontius (1988) speculates that there may be behaviors which humans are unable to control even when the likely consequences are clearly adverse. Research indicates that in a few people there are two types of limbic system dysfunctions which may lead to various types of behavior and perpetration: temporal lobe epilepsy and limbic psychotic trigger reaction (LPT). Limbic psychotic trigger reaction indicates an imbalance between the frontal lobes and the limbic system, causing lapses which may include hallucinogenic type states so that the person is no longer in control of his or her behavior.

The intergenerational transmission of abuse is also an important ingredient in understanding learned behavior as it relates to abuse and neglect. Korbin (1989) found 78 percent of the women studied who were in prison for fatal maltreatment of children had themselves been abused and victimized as children. Krugman (1987) argues that the pivotal nature of object relations theory, as it is applied to victimization, involves the range of reactions experienced by the victim with primary elaboration as a biphasic alternation between intrusion and denial. The secondary elaboration, however, addresses adaptation to traumatization often experienced by the victim. The result is that traumatization leads the individual to avoid intimacy and engaging in effective interpersonal relations.

Unresolved traumatic experiences are thought to impair the object relational world of victimized persons in adulthood and has direct applicability to experiences victims of physical and sexual abuse often relate. Veltkamp, Miller, and Silman (1994) discuss the vulnerability experienced as a child victim of sexual abuse. Adults who are victims of child sexual abuse may often harbor unconscious desires to relive earlier traumatic experiences and make these events demonstrate a different, varied, or perhaps more positive outcome. In this sense, they accommodate the psychopathology which often results in maladaptive patterns of behavior.

VICTIM–VICTIMIZER SPECTRUM

Numerous studies indicate that violent behavior has been learned and rewarded over time. The abuser learns to respond to all emotionally distressing cues with anger and violent behavior. In addition, learned helplessness theory predicts that the perception of helplessness can be learned during childhood. These two theories indicate that victims may proceed down two pathways:

1. They may become victimizers. They have learned violent behavior, have identified with the aggressor, or have learned that becoming violent themselves is a way of protecting themselves from feelings of vulnerability and helplessness, or
2. They may proceed down a path of continued victimization through adolescence and into adulthood. The best predictor of future violence is a history of past violent behavior.

Cases involving women who were battered in their relationships with men indicate that in these batterers' families of origin, the overwhelming majority showed a childhood history of battering and physical punishment. Physical punishment teaches that hitting is a characteristic in intimate relationships and teaches the child that the person who loves you the most has the right to hit you, which explains the carryover into adult violence. This also reflects the multigenerational pattern of abuse (see Figure 7.2).

MEASURES IN ASSESSING PERPETRATORS

There has been an increased effort to develop psychometrically acceptable measures. The following include, but are not limited to, current measures seen as developed with reference to the abuse syndrome and a sensitivity to abuse specific conditions.

- *Trauma Symptom Inventory* (Briere and Runtz, TSC-33; 1989): This measure is a brief abuse oriented instrument of psychometric quality that is used in clinical research as a measure of trauma impact. It is considered for use in assessing the long-term effects of child abuse. The TSC-33 yields five subscale scores: (1) anxiety, (2) depression, (3) dissociation, (4) postsexual abuse trauma, and (5) sleep disturbance. The measure yields a total score and

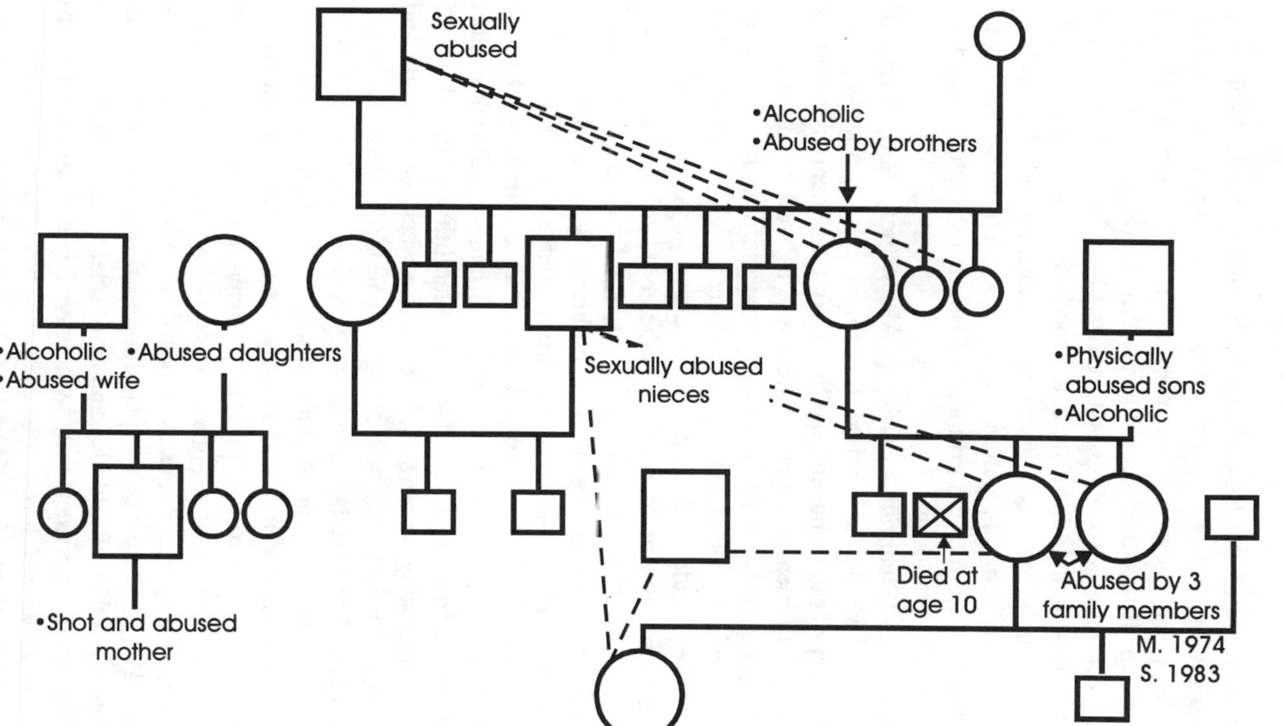

Figure 7.2 Pattern of Multigenerational Abuse

has been shown to demonstrate both validity and reliability in a variety of studies (Megana, 1990). Briere and Runtz (1992), Bagley (1989), identified weaknesses in the TSC-33 include: (1) the sleep disturbance subscale has limited reliability (alpha = .66); (2) there is some ambiguity regarding the content validity of the postsexual abuse trauma-hypothesized subscale (PSAT-H), which is seen as a measure of sexual abuse trauma; (3) there is no subscale within the TSC-33 that measures sexual difficulties, despite the prominence of such symptoms in adults molested as children.

- *Child Abuse Potential Inventory* (CAP; Milner, 1980): The CAP inventory is a screening device that measures a person's potential for physical abuse. The Child Abuse Potential Inventory attempts to measure parent pathology, as well as interactional difficulties that are related to physical child abuse. The CAP inventory asks subjects to agree or disagree with statements that have been made to discriminate between physical abusers and nonabusers. Factors derived from the abuse scale, describe psychological difficulties such as stress, rigidity, and unhappiness in interpersonal problems, i.e., problems with child and self, problems with family, problems from others. Validity and reliability data reveal that the CAP abuse scale reliability (KR-20) ranges from .91 to .96 for a variety of controls, at risk neglect and abuse groups, and test–retest reliabilities from .91 to .75 for control subjects across one-day, one-week, one-month, and three-month intervals, respectively. The CAP abuse scale has been found to correlate significantly with psychological factors such as external locus of control, poor ego strength, life hassles, life stress, depression, and anxiety, tension, and instability.
- *The Childcare Attitude Inventory* (Jones and Fay, 1988): This 80-item inventory is designed to assess adults potential for providing quality child care as opposed to neglectful and abusive care. The inventory is a paper-and-pencil measure, which measures a number of attitudes and emotional states that have been differentiated between adults who have healthy, constructive interactions with children from those who have unhealthy, destructive interactions (Jones and Fay, 1988). A 5-point Likert-type scale is used in the assessment of childcare attitudes. The specific

dimensions measured by this scale include (1) emotional stability; (2) expectations of children; (3) tolerance of attitudes toward child abuse; (4) explanations of child abuse. A factor analyzed study confirmed the presence of four specific factors, a Spearman-Brown split half (odd vs. even) reliability coefficient realized .91. The Childcare Attitude Inventory has shown a relationship effect with the Child Abuse Potential Inventory ($R = -.88$, $p < .001$), suggesting that adults with better childcare potential exhibited lower child abuse potential.

TREATMENT INTERVENTIONS FOR PERPETRATORS

There are several theoretical approaches to understanding interventions for perpetrators, the most common of which include educational and psychoeducational approaches, cognitive behavioral approaches, and legal initiatives. Programs that address treatment of perpetrators have not received rigorous review, and research on the short and long-term effects of these interventions. What is known is that psychoeducational techniques utilized with perpetrators, both male and female, are based on the belief that the understanding and management of power and control is essential in addressing perpetrator behavior. Cognitive–behavioral approaches to treatment of perpetrators have been used in an effort to address dysfunctional thought patterns than may underlie behavior that leads to violence and abuse (Edelson, 1985). This form of treatment addresses specific perpetrator behaviors, and attempts to define those behaviors that identify dysfunctional thought patterns and build cognitive and behavioral skills that reduce or eliminate the probability of perpetrator behaviors. Most cognitive behavioral forms of treatment include group-oriented approaches, anger management, techniques, and skill deficit conflict resolution. The anger management component encourages resocialization and skill development for the perpetrator in addressing the use of anger and violence in response to precipitating forms of behavior. Skill-deficit conflict resolution attempts to provide perpetrators with skills in resolving conflicts and proficiency in effectively communicating with others (Fagan and Browne, 1993).

Prevention and intervention strategies adopt the public health model, which focuses on preventing the spread of abuse by:

1. Eliminating the development of abusive behavior;
2. Strengthening and empowering potential victims to resist or avoid victimization;
3. Altering the environment that promotes violence and leads to abuse.

Several key factors must address prevention and intervention. These include:

- Early identification of people at risk
- Increased expectation for primacy prevention through behavioral change
- Improved models of coping with chronicity
- Self-identification of at-risk behaviors
- Public disclosure of at-risk status
- Legal and judicial confrontation of at-risk status
- Implemented life-style changes

Curbing the development of abusive behavior includes ways in which to reeducate potential high-risk abusers, so they learn to avoid the socialization patterns or triage of the abusive behaviors from childhood on. Furthermore, prevention programs need to support the empowerment of victims to resist harm if they are exposed or subjected to abuse. Community programs that address these preventive measures must be addressed to two groups: Those at high risk for being abused, who need to receive special inoculations designed to lower their risk, and those who are at high risk for being abusers who need to be fully educated and committed to their own behavioral change. Developing these models of prevention and intervention may reduce the effects of abuse, as well as the psychological impact of abusive situations. Religious and community programs designed to strengthen and empower healthy families also must be a key part of primary prevention, as is legislation to limit societal access of potential perpetrators to violence results in abusive types of behavior.

The criminal justice system has developed a series of programs that attempt to address dysfunctional thinking in perpetrators and that decrease violent responses that involve a spectrum of psychopathological disorders, including obsessive–compulsive disorder, depression, anxiety, and low self-esteem.

According to Walker (1979), the attitudes and values of those who treat perpetrators and offenders should include the following standards of competencies, attitudes, and values:

- Develop support for the women who have been victimized while treating their victimizer.
- Willingness to challenge stereotypical myths about battering relationships; for example, via accepting the reality of generational abuse.
- A cooperative and untangled bureaucracy to assist victims.
- Help for victims to enable them to deal with their own fear of violence.
- Multidisciplinary teams to evaluate and treat both victims and offenders.
- Develop an understanding of how institutions oppress and reinforce victimization (e.g., harassment).
- Development of healthy outlets for their own anger.
- Develop the ability to tolerate anger in others.
- Treatment programs to reassure the victim in working through the issues of victimization.
- Respect and belief in a person's capacity to change and to benefit from treatment.

8

Abuse, Harassment, and Violence in the Workplace

Sexual harassment, physical abuse, sexual abuse, work related injuries, and the exploitation of children, minorities, and physically and mentally challenged individuals, are some of the major causes of stress in the workplace.

Acts of violence, whether physical, psychological, or sexual are a major part of the fabric of workplace stress. The hearings to decide whether Clarence Thomas should or should not become an Associate Justice of the Supreme Court brought increased public attention to sexual harassment in particular as an issue in the workplace. What brought special interest to the hearings was the fact that Thomas was Chairman of the Equal Employment Opportunity Commission (EEOC). It is estimated that as many as 20,000 sexual harassment claims may be filed in a given year and two-thirds reach some level of administrative settlement. Although males as well as females are sexually harassed, women file more than 90 percent of the claims filed with the EEOC (Kenney, 1993; Stuitz, 1994).

Sexual harassment is typically perpetrated by people who have power over their victims and this formulates just one of the spectrum of issues related to violence in the workplace. Some managerial models and technological advances that have been realized in the work environment, along with a society which appears to continue to press for speed and efficiency, provide a variety of stressors that may lead to abuse, exploitation, and violence in the workplace. Table 8.1 summarizes some of the job related, psychological, and environmental factors that contribute to workplace problems. These factors together with the elements recognized by the International Society for Research on Aggression comprise some etiological issues relevant to understanding the broader spectrum of workplace stress and various forms of violence.

Table 8.1 Potential Exploitation and Abuse Factors in the Workplace

Job-Related Factors	Psychological Factors	Environmental Factors
Unfair promotional practices	Harassment	Excessive noise
	Feeling hopeless or bored	Nonsupportive management
Intimidating, demanding management styles	Too much or too little to do	Unfair rating procedures
Conflicts with coworkers or supervisors	Low self-esteem	No change of routine
Feeling overwhelmed by work	Highly self-critical	Failure to receive feedback or recognition
Lacking support from management	Lost sense of purpose	Unsafe working conditions
Glass ceiling	Overwhelmed	Overcrowded conditions
	Feeling not in control	Conflicts between employees
	Excessive work or job changes	Violation of child labor laws
	Communication difficulties	
	Verbal abuse	
	Passive–aggressive management style	

The Centers for Disease Control and Prevention (CDC) have established an epidemiological branch to address issues of workplace stress and violence. Their findings have been incorporated into the *Healthy People 2000* guidelines (CDC, 1991). This national policy includes several objectives specifically addressing the problems of violence, in particular job related and environmental factors. There are, however, other considerations that must be realized in assessing the potential for incursions upon the human rights of others. Researchers (Kenney, 1993) have explored the issues of violence and aggression. There are a set of theories that argue many abusive behaviors are learned through observation of familial, subcultural, and media events, and as a result of this are imitated. Examples of these behaviors include sexual harassment, exploitation, and abuse of minorities, abuse of individuals who may be mentally challenged, and physical and sexual violence in the workplace. It is these behaviors that underlie most violations of human rights. In addition to the learned aspect of these various forms of aggression, one must be conscious of the concept of economic inequality. Based on the notion of economic inequality, some forms of this aggression can generate feelings of hostility, resentment, and potential for violence. Economic inequality is not determined solely by median wages but as a function of the accessibility to valued resources, thus issues discussed in Table 8.1 such as job related factors (unfair promotional practices, intimidating management styles, conflicts with other workers, issues related to the glass ceiling) can all contribute to the potential for occupational violence and risks which take the form of harassment, exploitation, and abuse.

HARASSMENT, ABUSE, AND EXPLOITATION

The politics of the workplace are a key ingredient in understanding how harassment, abuse, and exploitation are interpreted. At the core are issues related to power and control and this often becomes entwined in the politics of harassment. In most cases it is the person who has the administrative or managerial position, the position of power and control who is most likely to face charges of harassment. While fewer women than men hold management positions in American society, the numbers of female executives and supervisors are beginning to show a trend upward. The EEOC has suggested a series of guidelines that may be beneficial for any individual who is in such a position:

1. Treat all human beings with dignity and respect.
2. Be especially aware of subordinate roles and both the verbal and nonverbal communications.
3. Always maintain a professional posture.
4. Don't refer to body parts.
5. If it involves more than shaking hands, don't do it.
6. Refrain from joking about sexual, humorous issues.
7. Be sensitive to all minor complaints.

STRESS AS A FACTOR IN THE WORKPLACE

Hans Selye defined stress as a nonspecific response to any demand. While some individuals restrict their definition of stress to personal catastrophes such as life-threatening illnesses, others include an array of events that, if they are to occur, require a significant change in an individual's ongoing life pattern. Stressful life events can be negative in the sense that they are usually socially undesirable. Such events may include frequent job reassignments, unexpected expectations of supervisors, or promotional practices perceived as unfair by the worker. Events such as anniversaries related to hiring and other significant work-related events, and promotions, which are socially desired and therefore seen as positive, also include stress. In cases of both "good" and "bad" stress the individual must adapt to the effects of the stress on their lives in the workplace.

The impact of stressful life events varies from person to person, and there are numerous theories that attempt to explain how an individual processes such stress. Some theories suggest that stress can cause various disorders or psychopathology while others argue that stress can be beneficial to employee productivity and morale. One theory, the victimization model, suggests that an event or series of events can cause psychopathology to occur in an otherwise healthy person. This view is based on research in extreme situations which include life-threatening experiences. For example, workers who become victims of industrial accidents that result in physical and psychological injury: Though these workers may have been otherwise healthy for their entire lives, they may now experience troubling recollections of the accident which could lead to anxiety or depression.

The predisposition theory suggests that stress results from genetic factors that influence a person's tolerance level and ability to adjust to workplace situations. For example, biochemical imbalances in the brain may result in poor adaptation to occupational skills needed and to competencies. Another theory suggests an additive burden, which contrasts in a number of ways with the vulnerability model. The additive burden model argues that personal dispositions and social conditions make independent causal contributions to the occurrence of psychopathology and the worker. It is also one that argues that the accumulation of small issues and problems in the workplace may result in emotional discomfort and distress. With the additive burden theory, the person begins to accumulate additional responsibilities and obligations to the point of burnout. Within the work setting the individual either internalizes these burdens or may express them in a more formidable way through violent acting out potential. Changes in benefits or loss of employment may predispose an individual to respond in a more violent way. It is important that health care providers be alert to the signs and symptoms of instability that may result in violent behavior. Some of these signs include but are not limited to the following:

1. Anger and tension in both speech and behavior
2. Agitation and restlessness
3. Argumentativeness
4. Defiance
5. Making threats with some clearly defined goal and objective
6. Paranoid ideation
7. Use of profanity
8. Speaking in a loud voice
9. Defensive behavior and attitude

The chronic burden theory places less emphasis on the influence of short-term stressful life experiences, suggesting instead that individuals adjust to stress or chronic situations over a longer period of time. The accumulated stress and chronic burden has both psychological and physical effects on the individual in the workplace. The victim of a chronic burden syndrome experiences repeated job related factors and psychological factors that were earlier discussed in Table 8.1. The victim of chronic burden syndrome may also begin to show physical symptoms of stress that include fatigue, headaches, increased consumption of alcohol, nicotine, or caffeine, sleep disturbance, avoidance or withdrawal from others, moodiness and irritability, and feelings of hopelessness in the workplace. Results of such physical symptoms and the chronicity of the disorder may result in the development of physical problems such as hypertension, heart disease, or cerebral vascular accident resulting in incapacitation and the need for long-term medical treatment.

JOB RELATED INTERVENTION AND PREVENTION

Prevention is a primary goal of managing the broad spectrum of occupational problems that cause job related stress. No workplace is immune to the potential factors summarized that can result in exploitation and abuse. The Centers for Disease Control has recommended that employers and researchers take active steps to prevent any of these factors and promote occupational health. They have encouraged the prompt development and implementation of prevention strategies but have encouraged training for early recognition and prompt intervention to avoid serious consequences. In addition, they have welcomed the presence of employee assistance programs to address the needs of employees facing stress in the workplace. Prevention strategies can be summarized as follows:

1. Challenges to occupational health are multicausal and continue to escalate significantly as the use and complexity of technology increases and demands on the worker for higher levels of productivity affect the human organism's ability to accommodate such change.
2. Specialists capable of dealing with workplace trauma can contribute to workplace order through a greater understanding of how to collect, recognize, identify, and provide crisis intervention so that the chronicity of problems is reduced or eliminated.
3. Prevention is best served through improved communication between management and workers. Addressing the broad spectrum of abuse and exploitation from a public health perspective will

ensure that attention is given to the multifaceted influences that trigger the various forms of abuse and exploitation in the workplace.

EMPLOYEE RESPONSIBILITIES

Employees must recognize the sources of job related stress and that this often includes their own attitude toward work and whether they believe that work is meaningful to their lives. Difficulties in upper management, advances in computerized technology, conflicts with co-workers, and difficulty in adapting to work routine, are all sources of job related stress. Stress most often shows itself through moodiness and irritability, through withdrawal from involvement in work activities and from fellow employees. It also shows itself through sleep difficulty, through decreased eye contact, fewer conversations, and increased consumption of substances of abuse including alcohol, caffeine, and nicotine as a form of coping or self-medication.

If one is to manage stress one must begin with individual employees assuming responsibility and control for both their minds and bodies and keeping themselves in a state of readiness for the demands of the work environment. The following issues are important for managing stressful life events and should be a regular part of the employee's life-style:

1. Nutrition and Health: Practicing good nutrition and understanding food groups and the appropriate balance for one's personal health will help in stress management.
2. Sleep: Close to one-quarter of the nation's population suffers from some form of sleep disturbance. An adequate amount of sleep and an understanding of the sleep cycle and its importance is a key component to stress management in the workplace.
3. Weight control: Overweight individuals are at high risk for a variety of diseases and conditions including high blood pressure, stroke, diabetes, coronary problems, and kidney and gallbladder diseases.
4. Smoking: Individuals who smoke require roughly 50 percent more health care services than nonsmokers. Some people think smoking

relieves stress, but research tends to suggest that the combination of smoking and stress produces a greater load on the cardiovascular system than either smoking or stress alone.

5. Physical exercise: Many corporations encourage Wellness Programs making it easy for employees to keep stress in check. Physical exercise when integrated into one's life-style relieves stress and tension and contributes to health and weight management.
6. Alcohol abuse: Alcoholism is a key factor in the workplace. More than 10 million problem drinkers are at risk for poor productivity or absenteeism, factors that further contribute to stress for both employees and managers.
7. Family and workplace issues: There are numerous issues related to the potential for abuse, exploitation, and harassment from the perspective of employee productivity as it interfaces with family life. High risk areas for family stress in the workplace include but are not limited to role overload and interference issues related to dual career conflicts. Also, time management problems and parenting stressors play a key role in this particular area. When the demands of one or more roles exceed the individual's capability to handle such roles, overload may occur. As a result, the individual's work and family expectations are contradictory and the demands on time and energy require the individual to address a multiplicity of demands and expectations. Among thosc factors influencing family issues and work productivity are the following:

a. Issues related to child care, including problems of day care, latchkey children, and emergencies involving the child.
b. Issues of child development ranging from preschool children through adolescence.
c. Parent and adolescent conflicts which include peer pressure, testing limits, drug and alcohol use and abuse, and teenage sexual activity.
d. School and academic activities which conflict with parents' work schedules.

Managing stress in the workplace is the responsibility of both employers and employees and begins with creating a healthy individual and a healthy work environment. Several strategies may be of benefit to addressing workplace stress. These include the following:

1. Carefully assess everyday life stressors in the workplace.
2. Develop a plan to resolve each stressor one at a time and manage them in an effective and identified way.
3. Seek assistance through professional counseling and employee assistance programs in an effort to develop strategies toward successful management.
4. Employ various stress management skills and techniques often provided by licensed professionals in trying to cope with stressful employment situations.
5. Utilize relaxation skills and deep breathing exercises to relieve tension.
6. Understand one's own stress–performance ratio and find the balance between underload and overload.
7. Person-centered managers who seek to gain the input and ideas of workers in addressing workplace stress will find pathways to conflict resolution.
8. Help to create an atmosphere that encourages openness with respect to decision making, and develop a written plan of how to assess and achieve each of the needs one has in the workplace.

As we enter the twenty-first century, there is a realization that we are in a period of more rapid growth and expansion in workplace efficiency and the use of advanced technology. As a consequence our society will have a highly mobile, fast-paced, and frequently detached workforce. This will challenge the individual's ability to accommodate and assimilate into their life and personalities challenges to be faced in a changing work environment. Of crucial importance to this is an understanding on the parts of both management and worker that exploitation and abuse in the workplace be addressed, understood, and steps taken to prevent its reoccurrence. The extent to which we educate, understand, and work toward prevention of sexual harassment, verbal harassment, workplace exploitation, and abuse is the extent to which we can expect a workforce to maintain both high productivity and morale.

9

Persons with Disabilities: Issues of Abuse and Exploitation in the Workplace

Allan L. Beane, Ph.D.

INTRODUCTION

According to Lesley Wright and Marti Smye (1996, p. 13), authors of *Corporate Abuse,* "throughout history, abuse has been the norm, not the exception, in work relationships." Workers are abused by corporations, their supervisors, and their coworkers. Even though laws have been passed to protect individuals, very little has been written about how to prevent and intervene in abusive work environments, especially when individuals with disabilities are involved.

Perhaps no law has been so far reaching as the Americans with Disabilities Act (ADA) of 1990. This law has helped some individuals secure jobs and has helped some receive the accommodations they need in order to be productive employees. However, there are still concerns regarding the number of jobs being secured, the types of jobs secured, the opportunities for advancement, and the social acceptance of individuals with disabilities.

ADA was passed because organizations were intentionally excluding employees with disabilities from the workplace. Now that they are entering the workforce in greater numbers, they may encounter abuse, exploitation, and outright intentional exclusion *within* the workplace. Some of them have been physically integrated into the workplace, but not socially integrated. They do not feel accepted by their coworkers and they do not have a sense of belonging in the organization. Of those responding to the Harris Poll, 33 percent said they were encountering unfavorable attitudes in the workplace, less than half said they felt they were treated as equals and most said others simply "felt sorry or embarrassed for them" (Medgyesi, 1996). Attitudinal barriers they face are often greater and more difficult to change than the barriers of facilities. They currently have greater access to jobs but face the less visible but real obstacles presented by the negative attitudes of coworkers.

The importance of successful social integration must not be underestimated. According to Florian (1978), successful rehabilitation is achieved when a person with disabilities is *accepted* as a worker in the open job market. Feeling accepted by coworkers and having a sense of belonging impacts the individual's mental health, physical health, relationships, and behavior inside and outside the work environment. Therefore, name-calling, teasing, harassment, and intentional social isolation should be considered abusive behaviors.

When seeking to promote the acceptance of employees with disabilities, it is important to be sensitive to all possible contributing factors.

POSSIBLE CONTRIBUTING FACTORS

Employees with disabilities may experience abuse for the same reasons as nondisabled employees. Their disabilities may appear to be the reasons they are not accepted when, in fact, there are several interacting contributing factors. The following is a brief discussion of the factors that may contribute to their abuse. Such factors are restraining forces and barriers which inhibit efforts to change the attitudes, thinking, and behaviors of coworkers. Therefore, it is important to consider these factors when developing a program for promoting the social acceptance of employees with disabilities. Some of the possible contributing factors are:

1. *Perceived Cause of Disability.* When the cause of a disability is viewed as external to the individual, he or she is viewed as more productive and more likely to work a long time in the organization (Bordieri and Drehmer, 1987).
2. *Perceived Disruption in Social Interaction.* Albrecht, Walker, and Levy (1982) found that the perceived degree of disruption in social interaction was a stronger contributor than the perception that the person was responsible for his or her disability.
3. *Physical Characteristics and Innate Preferences.* Attractive individuals are more likely to receive assistance when they need help and more likely to secure jobs (ABC News, 1995). Many employees with disabilities are considered deficient in appearance.
4. *Poor Social History.* The quality of the interactions experienced by individuals influence their ability to be accepted by others (Asher and Coie, 1990).
5. *Comfort Zone.* Some employees may engage in behavior to remain in an inferior and dependent position and encourage their own social isolation (Derman and Hauge, 1994).
6. *Overly Aggressive Behavior.* An adult who is overly aggressive may not be accepted by his or her coworkers or he or she may take the lead role in the abuse of others (Byrne, 1993).
7. *Temperament.* An employee with a "hot-headed" temperament is more likely to be aggressive with other employees than an employee who has a calm temperament.
8. *Disruptive Behavior.* When employees are off-task and cause others to be off-task, they are considered a nuisance. It does not take long for coworkers to communicate their intolerance for such behavior. In fact, employees may be less tolerant of individuals with disabilities.
9. *Withdrawal.* Individuals who are "withdrawn" may be treated as abnormal (Morris, 1994, p. 62).

10. *Lack of Social Skills.* There is a strong relationship between social ability and social acceptance (Oden, 1981). When employees are markedly lacking in social skills, they stand out from their coworkers and may become targets of abuse.
11. *Poor Family Environment.* Employees living in the midst of aggression and violence, often take their fears, anger, and aggressions to work.
12. *Expectations and Reputation.* Because abused individuals often have low social self-esteem, they may not expect success and tend to behave in a manner consistent with their own expectations and the expectations of others. An employee's reputation as being a rejected person may not cause more abuse, but it certainly maintains it and makes striving for acceptance difficult.
13. *Stigmas.* Nathaniel Floyd (1987) says that victims of abuse become stigmatized. A stigma is an attribute that is deeply discrediting and reduces the possessor in the minds of others from a whole and usual person to a tainted, discounted one (Goffman, 1963, reported in Katz, 1981). Individuals with disabilities have a long history of stigmatization.
14. *Responses to Abuse.* An employee's reaction to abuse may cause further abuse. Once an employee is rejected, he or she may engage in inappropriate behavior (e.g., aggression, withdrawal) that further encourages rejection and other forms of abuse.
15. *Personality Type (Too Sensitive).* According to Byrne (1994, p. 21), the personality type which puts a person most at risk of abuse is the shy, sensitive type. Such individuals tend to take everything to heart and personalize all negative comments. This overaction encourages abuse.
16. *Lack of Skills with Social Value.* Employees with disabilities may be abused because they do not have the same interests and/or skills as their coworkers.
17. *Prejudice.* One of the most obvious causes of abuse in the workplace is prejudice. Prejudice toward individuals with disabilities has been well documented (Kilbury, Bordileri, and Wong, 1996).
18. *Protecting Self-esteem by Avoiding Attribute Associations.* Some employees may seek to protect their self-image by restricting their range of contacts with dissimilar (or perceived as dissimilar) people (Kidder and Stewart, 1975). They may even view intervening

for abused employees as risky to their own social standing and fear they may become targets.

19. *Fear.* According to Hall (1995), everyone has at least five fears: (1) fear of being laughed at; (2) fear of losing what one has; (3) fear of abuse; (4) fear of the unknown; and (5) fear of exposure (weaknesses, etc.). These fears tend to control behavior. In fact, employees may engage in rejecting behavior in order to protect themselves from one or more of the five fears.
20. *Jealousy.* When coworkers are viewed as possessing something that seems to be beyond the reach of other employees, jealousy rules the work environment.
21. *Need for Security and Safety.* Another possible reason employees mistreat others is their need to feel safe and secure when faced with the unfamiliar or uncertain. In their familiar world of friends and surroundings, employees find security. Therefore, when confronted with someone who looks different, who behaves differently, or who holds different beliefs, the tendency is to "put them down" to avoid interacting with the unfamiliar.
22. *Self-Centeredness and Lack of Sensitivity.* Some employees are egocentric. Self-centered attitudes do not produce sensitivity toward others.
23. *For the Laughs.* Television has provided several models for getting "a good laugh." Some employees strive to get "a good laugh" from their coworkers by criticizing others.
24. *Ignorance.* It is difficult to imagine, but sometimes employees are unaware of the hurt they cause.
25. *Revenge.* Some employees mistreat others because they are being abused. Their feelings build up and are brought to work where they are expressed upon employees who are perceived as weaker.
26. *Peer Group Needs a Target.* By rejecting others, work groups define the boundaries of their acceptance in order to bring unity to the group.
27. *Poor Health, Self-Esteem and Poor Self-confidence.* Some researchers have found individuals who mistreat others to have positive self-esteem with a high dose of self-confidence. More and more people are feeling that individuals who engage in violent behavior have positive self-esteem. However, other researchers believe that when these individuals are also victims (perhaps at

home) they have feelings of inadequacy and displace their feelings onto employees who are more vulnerable.

28. *Reaction to Tension.* Workplaces are often environments with considerable tension. Inappropriate employee behavior becomes an outlet for tensions.

29. *Aggression is Allowed and Rewarded.* Abuse occurs because it is allowed to occur. In some work environments, little or nothing may be done to stop the abuse of others. Employees may also see reinforcing value in mistreating others. For example, in some work environments they gain some popularity through their behavior and get what they want, which is power and control.

30. *Desire for Power and Control.* Employees who mistreat others thirst for power and control. Therefore, they are usually stronger than average and their victims are usually weaker than average.

31. *Contributing Factors Related to Work Environment.* Unsatisfactory work environment factors may also contribute to the abuse of employees. The following may be contributing factors: (a) low staff morale; (b) high employee turnover; (c) unclear standards of behavior; (d) inconsistent methods of discipline; (e) poor organization; (f) inadequate supervision; (g) employees not treated as valued individuals; (h) unrealistic expectations; (i) not enough appropriate equipment to complete tasks; (j) lack of support for new employees; (k) intolerance of differences; (l) all employees arriving and leaving at once; (m) allowing hurtful graffiti to remain on walls and other public places; (n) atmosphere of destructive competition; (o) no clear procedures for reporting and dealing with abusive incidents; (p) abusive behavior is ignored by personnel; (q) lack of supervision in isolated/hidden areas (in and between buildings); (r) crowded and narrow dark halls; (s) crowded locker rooms; (t) lack of support for employees with disabilities; (u) supervisors who use sarcasm and humiliate employees in front of coworkers; and (v) no *Acceptance of Diversity Policy.*

PREVENTION AND INTERVENTION RECOMMENDATIONS/STRATEGIES

The abuse and exploitation of employees with disabilities can be a problem requiring one or two solutions or it can be a multifaceted problem requiring several solutions. In fact, no *single* strategy is going to be as effective as the systematic implementation of several strategies. Even though ADA states that employers cannot segregate employees with disabilities from other employees (Vernon-Oehmke, 1994), very little attention has been given to strategies for promoting their social acceptance and preventing their abuse and exploitation. To effectively tackle the problem of abuse of adults in the workplace, Beane (1996) developed more than 100 prevention and intervention recommendations/strategies that are system-centered, personnel-centered, coworker-centered, and employee-centered. These strategies go beyond common courtesy and etiquette and focus on changing policies and procedures, changing the attitudes, thinking, and behavior of the leadership and coworkers, as well as providing assistance to individuals who are abused or who are at risk of being abused. All of the strategies and their rationale cannot be discussed in this chapter; however, the following is a sampling of the strategies. Some of the recommendations are creative ideas generated during brainstorming sessions, but are well grounded in the realities of the work environment and the needs of persons with disabilities. Many of the strategies are based on sound research and can be implemented quickly with little effort. Some of the strategies are being applied to the workplace for the first time.

Summary Listing of System-Centered Strategies

To effectively promote the social acceptance of employees with disabilities, the organization must walk-its-talk. This requires a careful examination of its policies, procedures, and programs. Therefore, the organization's leadership should be encouraged by psychologists, sociologists, counselors and others to:

1. Establish a *people first* policy. All communications must reflect the importance of considering the employee with a disability as a person first. All communications should say, "employees with disabilities," not "disabled employees." Terms such as *retarded, spastic, slow, midget, dwarf, unfortunate, afflicted, diseased, crippled, lame,* should never be used.
2. Provide employees with training regarding the nature and needs of employees with disabilities and the Americans with Disabilities Act of 1990 (ADA).

3. Provide supervisory personnel with opportunities to discuss their thoughts and concerns with others who have had experience supervising employees with disabilities. Employees with disabilities should also participate in the discussions.
4. Examine current policies and procedures that are placing employees with disabilities in embarrassing situations.
5. Communicate commitment to providing a physically and psychologically safe environment for all employees.
6. Establish and enforce a code-of-conduct and behavioral contracts. The code-of-conduct should include content focusing on name-calling, teasing, harassment, social isolation, and other forms of abuse.
7. Establish an *anonymous hotline/helpline* or some other procedure for reporting incidences of abuse and exploitation.
8. Educate employees to be more sensitive and concerned about the well-being of others.
9. Harness the energy of all employees and ask them to help the organization develop and implement a plan for making the organization a *caring workplace.*
10. Purchase books and subscribe to newsletters and magazines that promote sensitivity and tolerance/acceptance in the workplace.

Summary Listing of Personnel-Centered Strategies

The organization's leadership personnel have a tremendous influence on the attitudes of coworkers. Since they quickly communicate their anxieties, their fears, and their acceptance, they should be encouraged to continuously assess the messages they are communicating through their own day-to-day attitudes and behavior (verbal and nonverbal). Therefore, the organization's leadership should be encouraged by psychologists, sociologists, counselors and others to:

1. Examine their own attitudes toward employees with disabilities and be sensitive to negative self-talk regarding these employees. They should identify and eliminate their own biases and prejudices.
2. Give appropriate eye contact to employees with disabilities.

3. Avoid favoritism.
4. Warn employees with disabilities of changes in procedures and structure (e.g., furniture arrangement, schedules, routines).
5. Develop *with-it-ness.* The leadership should be sensitive to the tone of the social interactions of employees and be alert to nonverbal signals that may indicate interpersonal problems and abusive behaviors. Rumors of abuse should also be investigated without making situations worse.
6. Examine their own self-esteem and strive to improve them. It is difficult for leaders to enhance the self-esteem of others when they have poor self-esteem.
7. Avoid mentioning how employees with disabilities are different (in a negative sense) from their parents and siblings.
8. Rid themselves of all belittling behavior such as shouting, sarcastic and insulting remarks, and hurtful teasing. The supervisory leadership should model accepting behavior.
9. Never seek to "over protect" employees with disabilities.

Summary Listing of Coworker-Centered Strategies

In addition to improving the attitudes, thinking, and behavior of the organization's leadership, it is also important to implement strategies that focus on impacting the attitudes, thinking, and behaviors of individuals working with employees with disabilities. Therefore, the organization's leadership should be encouraged by psychologists, sociologists, counselors and others to:

1. Use strategic job assignments to increase the employee's social contact with nondisabled employees. To facilitate their social integration, employees with disabilities should not be seated at the periphery of the work area.
2. Routinely take and display pictures of all employees working cooperatively (Joiner, Beane, and Grant, 1975).
3. Design job assignments which require group effort and reward cooperative behavior rather than the result (Joiner et al., 1975).
4. Prohibit negative comments from anyone regarding employees.

5. Engage several small groups of employees in a variety of service projects. The research findings of Sherif, Harvey, White, Hood, and Sherif (1961, reported in Asher and Coie, 1990, p. 179) support this recommendation. Requiring hostile parties to cooperate in order to achieve a mutual service goal resulted in more favorable attitudes and interactions among group members.
6. Avoid awarding special statuses or privileges to employees with disabilities, except when to do so is absolutely necessary (Joiner et al., 1975).
7. Provide effective illustrations and models of acceptance and discuss them with employees.
8. Discuss with employees national, state, or local incidences of discrimination, bigotry, and biases reported in the media.
9. Teach all employees the importance of positive *self-talk* about themselves and others.
10. Be aware of the weaknesses of employees and never ask them to display their weaknesses.

Summary List of Employee-Centered Strategies

The above strategies focused on the policies and procedures of the organization, the attitudes, thinking, and behaviors of the organization's leadership, and the attitudes and behaviors of coworkers. It is also important to implement strategies focusing on employees with disabilities. Therefore, the organization's leadership should be encouraged by psychologists, sociologists, counselors and others to:

1. Encourage employees with disabilities to "sample" a variety of potential coworkers as friends in order to identify those who can become suitable companions.
2. Arrange for new employees with disabilities to meet some of their coworkers in an informal social setting prior to starting work.
3. Help employees with disabilities to develop self-confidence and teach them to communicate this confidence. This will lessen the likelihood of them becoming a target. People also enjoy interacting with those who are confident.
4. Encourage employees with disabilities to have positive expectations regarding their own acceptance.

5. Enlist the assistance of all personnel who are acquainted with employees who are being rejected and abused. Ask them to call these individuals by name, to talk to them whenever possible, and to identify ways these employees can become active in the organization and feel like they belong.
6. Support employees with disabilities who wish to become more socially acceptable by developing normative appearances and behavior.
7. Teach employees with disabilities the importance of positive *self-talk* regarding themselves.
8. Teach employees with disabilities to use emotional rehearsals. When they face potentially abusive situations, it is best for them to think it through in advance and consider all of the possibilities.
9. Encourage employees with disabilities to openly talk about their abilities and disabilities.
10. Help overweight employees through wellness programs. They may be at risk of being socially rejected.

CONCLUSION

It is critical that organizations realize that crash courses are usually not effective. In order to effectively prevent the abuse and exploitation of employees, a plan is needed that uses strategies like those discussed in this chapter. Strategies from all four areas should be considered: (1) System-Centered Strategies, (2) Personnel-Centered Strategies, (3) Coworker-Centered Strategies, and (4) Employee-Centered Strategies. As Helen Keller said, "When we do the best we can, we never know what miracle is wrought in our life, or in the life of another."

10

Repression, Dissociation, and Recovered Memory

Considerable controversy has emerged in both the mental health and legal professions regarding repression, dissociation, and recovered memory. Some clinicians recognize repression as a real phenomenon and see a variety of clinical disorders including anxiety, depression, eating disorders, and sexual abuse and sexual dysfunction as being casually linked to repression of childhood abuse (Browne, 1991; Terr, 1995). Others have been cautious about and critical of both the likelihood and admissibility of repressed memory across the clinical and legal spectrum of mental health care (Pynoos & Nadar, 1989; Loftus, 1993; Freyd, 1996).

Adult survivors of childhood or adolescent abuse may retain memories of the abusive experiences (Davidson and Foa, 1991; Browne, 1992). Summit (1983) provides guidance in understanding the long-term aftereffects of childhood abuse through his sexual abuse accommodation syndrome. This model describes a constellation of conditions that offer a working model which allows clinicians to better evaluate and understand how an individual accommodates to the trauma resulting from sexual abuse. It is recognized that if the psychological symptoms that develop at the time of the abuse are untreated, they may remain dormant only to emerge at a later time in life, often with increased severity. Adults with childhood histories of abuse usually seek treatment for problems not always recognized as related to the history of abuse. That is, the symptoms that emerge often relate to anxiety, sleep disturbance, poor concentration, and fears of the impact of abusive relationships on their lives (Goldberger and Breznitz, 1993). Adult survivors of incest, as well as other forms of child abuse, often experience a variety of symptoms associated with posttraumatic stress disorder (PTSD).

The American Psychiatric Association's *Diagnostic and Statistical Manual* (DSM-IV; 1994a) suggests that some of the aftereffects of childhood abuse may not appear until adulthood. The diagnostic category of posttraumatic stress disorder (309.81) now suggests that a person who is exposed to a traumatic event must have (1) experienced, (2) witnessed, or (3) been confronted with an event that involved actual or threatened injury or threat to their physical integrity. As a result of having experienced intense fear, helplessness, or horror, the adult survivor of abuse may develop PTSD. While no one specific contributing factor can be associated with a delayed reaction in adult survivors of abuse, a consistent finding is that the long-term impact of abuse and the realization of this in later life often have a negative impact on individuals, including the phenomenon of repressed memory.

THEORETICAL CONSIDERATIONS IN RECOVERED MEMORIES

Highlighted here are some of the points that memory theory and research has raised in regard to assessment of recovered memories of childhood experiences that have included abuse and traumatization.

- Johnson, Hashprodie, and Lindsay (1993) have hypothesized that people have the experience of remembering when they associate current verbal events to the past. Numerous factors are thought to be involved in determining whether a mental event is experienced as a memory. Some people are more likely to experience an image or idea as a memory if they are trying to remember something when it comes to mind. Or, a vivid image is easily generated during an attempt to remember a traumatic event and is likely to be experienced as the memory (Whittlesea, 1993).

- Suggestibility can make an important contribution to memory source. Loftus and Coan (1995) examine evidence of the suggestibility of human memory and conclude that the same sort of process that contributes to false memories in laboratory studies can also lead to false memories of traumatic childhood experiences. Numerous factors contribute to the overall strength of suggestion, including the perceived authority and trustworthiness of the source, the perceived plausibility of the suggestions, and factors that lower the individual's memory-monitoring criteria. Furthermore, individuals are more likely to fall prey to suggestions about nonmemorable details than to suggestions regarding memorable autobiographical experiences (Loftus, 1993).
- Source monitoring involves awareness of uncertainty about the sources of given recollections individuals may have. Usually, we are able to identify the sources of our thoughts or images. Sometimes, however, conditions lead us to believe that an idea that we think is based on a memory of an actual event may actually reflect an unconscious conflict.
- Cognitive theorists feel a filing-system metaphor can be used wherein memory records can become incomplete or lost over time, and that general knowledge and expectation sometimes fill in the facts in the retrieval of memory and information that has been stored. In this file-storage model of memory, past thoughts and perceptions are represented by an internal code that is stored in some location or memory. A contrasting model argues a connectionist hypothesis in which information and memory is not stored in any one location but rather distributed across the network. This contrasting model argues that memories of similar events can interfere with one another, cue one another, or become blended together, resulting in a blurring of events and the capture of the accuracy of the memory.

In considering various models of remembering traumatic events, a preponderance of evidence suggests that the more memorable an event, the more difficult it would be to create false memories of that event. What seems most clear is what Lindsay and Reed (1995) have argued in addressing the issue of memory, work, and psychotherapy. These clinical researchers suggest that some approaches combine all of the factors known to increase suggestibility in memory work; that is, an authority figure who can be trusted; a rationale for plausible hidden memories; motivation for trying to recover such memories; repeated exposure to suggestive information from multiple sources; and techniques that enhance and enrich imagery and lower source-monitoring criteria.

The child sexual abuse accommodation syndrome serves as a model for understanding both the reason many adults are able to reveal child sexual abuse histories for the first time in therapy and also why they may not be believed. Adult survivors of child sexual abuse are often reluctant to share memories in therapy or may simply be unaware of the repressed traumatic experience. Thus, their presentation may range from only displaying symptoms to disclosing openly and clearly their corroborated memories of sexual abuse.

Popma (1995) examined the impact of a therapist's knowledge, experience, and attitudes about childhood sexual abuse and how effective those variables are in recognizing and conceptualizing proper treatment strategies for adult survivors of child sexual abuse. Results of this study demonstrated that increases in knowledge of child sexual abuse issues increased the therapist's perception of a client as a survivor, regardless of clarity of presentation. Furthermore, the more knowledgeable therapists were more apt to see child sexual abuse trauma as a main issue for therapy. Some differences between male and female psychologists were found in terms of the effects of years of experience on victim blame. More experience working with child sexual abuse survivors decreased victim blaming attitudes among women therapists but increased victim blaming attitudes among male therapists. Finally, increase in the clarity of the child sexual abuse presentation by the client increased the likelihood that symptoms consistent with PTSD would be chosen as the diagnosis for the client.

FALSE MEMORY SYNDROME

Bass and Davis (1988) report, "if you genuinely think you were abused and your life shows symptoms, there is a strong likelihood that you were" (p. 186). This publication has introduced an etiological phenomenon that has had very complex consequences in both the clinical treatment and the litigation field. The American Psychological Association (1995a) has convened a task force to address the numerous issues related to this and intends to release a series of statements on what is known about repressed memory and how accurate it believes the literature to be in this area. Also, recommendations will be made addressing both areas of clinical service and research in the areas of repressed memory.

The American Psychiatric Association (1994b) policy statement regarding memories of sexual abuse points out that all physicians must carefully avoid prejudicing the cause of a patient's difficulties or the veracity of the patient's reports. No clinician should exert pressure on patients to believe in events that may not have occurred nor encourage the patient to disrupt important relationships or make other important decisions based on these speculations. The American Psychiatric Association Board of Trustees noted that the problems separating false from true statements of abuse are compounded by the complex nature of memory itself. They also note that memories can be significantly influenced by questioning. They point out that human memory is a complex process about which there is a substantial base of scientific knowledge. Memory can be divided into four stages, including input or encoding, storage, retrieval, and recounting. These processes can be influenced by a variety of factors, including developmental stage expectations and knowledge base prior to an event. It is noted that some individuals who have experienced documented traumatic events may, nevertheless, include some inconsistent elements in their reports. In addition, hesitancy in making a report and recanting following the report can occur in victims of documented abuse. Therefore, these seemingly contradictory findings do not exclude the possibility that the report is based on a true event. In addition, memories can be significantly influenced by questions, especially in young children. It has also been shown that repeated questioning may lead individuals to report memories of events that never occurred. It is important for mental health professionals to maintain an empathic, nonjudgmental, neutral stance toward memories of sexual abuse. Many individuals who have experienced sexual abuse have a history of not being believed by their parents or others in whom they put their trust. Expressions of disbelief are likely to cause the patient further pain and decrease his or her willingness to seek treatment.

Recent estimates (American Psychological Association, 1995b) suggest that 16 percent of litigation relating to mental health claims involved repressed memories. These claims appear to fall into five categories:

1. The treating therapist is sued by the family member or person who is the alleged abuser. This is the most frequent type of case.
2. Repressed memories are a secondary issue to another cause of action, typically sexual misconduct or suicide.
3. The therapist is sued by the patient who now recants the repressed memories and alleges memory implantation by the therapist. These cases are growing in number.
4. Repressed memories are associated with cases of multiple victims in an institutional setting, although these cases are also relatively rare.
5. The prior treating therapist is the subject of repressed memories years after treatment has been terminated.

Litigation addressing repressed memory has noted a large number of cases filed in recent years based on memories of abuse recalled through psychotherapy. Much of this litigation has been facilitated by the legal doctrine known as the "Lay Discovery Rule." In civil cases, a lawsuit must be filed within a certain number of years following the event which might give rise to the lawsuit (i.e., the statute of limitations). While the limitations period varies from state to state, lawsuits alleging child sexual abuse typically must be filed within a three-year period after the victim reaches the age of majority. Courts have recognized the need for exceptions in certain cases where a plaintiff has no memory of an injury or its cause.

There are implications for the application of delayed discovery to repressed memories for health care providers. More specifically, the extent to which the therapist plays a role in uncovering the memories of alleged abuse in childhood that may be of a sexual nature, is the extent to which the therapist is likely to become the principal in a lawsuit which addresses the means by which this information came to consciousness. It is commonplace for some psychotherapists to use relaxation and clinical hypnosis to aid patients in addressing repressed memory issues of childhood sexual abuse. The therapist should be aware that the court may discount or disallow testimony from individuals whose memories were refreshed through the utilization of hypnosis or other techniques.

Repression is considered by some as one of the most extensive forms of dissociation, a process which involves the disruption of the normal connection between feelings, thoughts, behavior, and memories. When the disruption involves memory, the person does not have a recall of important events. Research studies have revealed that up to 60 percent of child sexual abuse survivors report incomplete or total absence of abuse specific memories at some time after their victimization.

With respect to the use of repressed memory as a part of addressing clinical issues related to child sexual abuse, several important practical considerations should be made by professionals and health care providers addressing this.

- Be cautious about assumptions and conclusions made through psychotherapy where there is no substantiation of fact.
- Carefully review with patients the risks of making public allegations regarding repressed memories of sexual abuse and potential consequences for family members or significant others.
- The specialized techniques in uncovering repressed memories should be used with extreme caution. Information gathered by means of techniques such as hypnosis, sodium amytal, or other techniques that may serve as an adjunct to therapeutic intervention may not be admissible in a court of law. Furthermore, such techniques often have limitations related to validity and reliability.
- Clinicians involved with services to patients claiming repressed memories should maintain objectivity and impartiality and avoid

advocacy roles related to recovering memories of childhood abuse.

- Clinicians should provide patients with informed consent prior to exploring repressed memories of child sexual abuse, and educate patients as to the controversy related to repressed memories.
- Clinicians should keep abreast of emerging empirical research related to repressed memory of child sexual abuse and its interface with therapeutic interventions and revelations.
- Clinical and legal developments regarding repressed memory related to child sexual abuse must be approached with clinical caution and from a professionally ethical position. The validity and reliability of repressed memories, the process by which repressed memories emerge, and the interface of repressed memories with stressful life events at certain ages and stages of life are subjects that need further continued clinical study and scientific investigation as well as further legal clarification.

The American Psychological Association has developed an interim report on adult memories of childhood sexual abuse experiences. The report's six basic conclusions:

1. Controversies about adult recollections should not obscure the fact that the child sexual abuse is a complex, pervasive problem in America that has historically been unacknowledged.

2. Most people who were sexually abused as children remember all or part of what happened to them. In a policy statement, the American Academy of Child and Adolescent Psychiatry (1990), in identifying guidelines for the clinical evaluation of child and adolescent sexual abuse, and considering the question of false allegations, points out: The possibility of false allegations needs to be considered, particularly if allegations are coming from a parent rather than a child, if parents are engaged in a dispute over custody or visitation, and/or if the child is a preschooler. Under such circumstances, a clinician should consider observing the child separately with each parent. Before these observations, the clinician should meet alone with the child to establish trust and ensure the child will feel some degree of control over the interview with the alleged offender. If the child is too upset by the proposed visits and there is a risk of traumatizing the child, the clinician may

decide that a visit with the alleged offender should not occur. Resistance from a parent alone is not a reason to avoid this part of the evaluation.

3. False allegations may arise in other situations as well, such as the misinterpretation of a child's statement or behavior by relatives or caregivers. Adolescents may also occasionally make false allegations out of vindictiveness or to cover their own sexual activity. Children who have experienced prior sexual abuse may sometimes misinterpret actions of adults or accuse the wrong person of abuse.

4. It is possible for incidents of abuse that have been forgotten for a long time to be remembered, although the mechanisms by which this might happen are not well understood.

5. It is possible to construct convincing psuedomemories for events that never occurred, although the mechanisms by which this occurs are not well understood.

6. There are gaps in knowledge about the processes that lead to accurate or inaccurate recollection of childhood sexual abuse.

The APA report also indicates the following statements which should guide not only the psychological profession but also the public in dealing with memories of childhood abuse:

1. Therapists must approach questions of childhood abuse from a neutral position. There is no single set of symptoms that automatically means that a person was a victim of childhood abuse.
2. The public is advised, when looking for a psychotherapist, to see a licensed practitioner who has training and experience in the issues for which treatment is sought.

Although many abused adults suffer significantly long-term effects, all adult survivors may not experience such severe reactions. The effects of abuse are highly individualized, because the circumstances of the abuse vary markedly, as do the personalities of both the victims and the perpetrators. It is well recognized that a history of child sexual abuse often coexists with a history of other types of abusive situations or other forms of family dysfunction. Some of the differences in the effects of the abuse may result from multiple sources of traumatization. The aftereffects of abuse are often a spectrum disorder and include a variety of psychopathology. A notable impact of abuse on victims is dissociation, which is seen as a major coping strategy used by children and adults in dealing with ongoing traumatization. The phenomenon of dissociation suggests that an individual may develop an ability to withdraw part or all of his or her consciousness from the circumstances of abuse. Dissociative reactions and disorders, beginning in childhood, have clearly been identified. Although some professionals believe that most individuals have the ability to dissociate, there are others who argue against this. Dissociative identity disorder suggests the presence of two or more distinct identities or personality states that take control of the person's behavior, wherein the victim is unable to recall important personal information that is too extensive to be explained by ordinary forgetfulness.

The adult survivor of abuse is often able to use dissociative reactions to protect him or herself from the reality of abuse and the painful experiences that sexual and other forms of abuse may provide. This process may persist into adulthood and be seen as one of the coping strategies the individual has adopted in order to be able to cope with the abuse experienced much earlier in life. Adult survivors often have memories that are accessible at times, and inaccessible at others. Such memory patterns have been identified and associated with repression or dissociation of trauma as a means of coping and protection. Repressed memories are especially needed strategies when abuse is not acknowledged or discussed and when the victim is left vulnerable to repeated episodes of abuse. Studies suggest that a period of forgetting abuse is not uncommon among victims and that as many as 40 percent of those reporting childhood sexual or nonsexual abuse report a period of forgetting some or all of the abuse that occurred.

SUMMARY

Adult survivors of abuse often have symptoms associated with a variety of disorders, including anxiety, depression, obsessive–compulsive disorder, and various personality disorders that are best conceptualized by theories of trauma reaction and PTSD. Adult survivors with long-term effects and delayed onset of symptoms must be recognized as individuals who are only beginning to uncover the psychological impact of the traumatizing experiences that took place much earlier in their lives. Efforts to address risk factors for abuse, neglect, and maltreatment must be an integrated part of prevention interventions. While abused children have a variety of initial and long-term psychological affective, cognitive, and behavioral effects, not all individuals demonstrate long-term effects from abuse.

The term *adult survivor* of child abuse can refer to any person who has experienced abuse as a child by a family member or significant others, but it most often refers to adults who experience the long-term effects of untreated and unresolved abuse from their childhood. The *adult nonsurvivor* is defined as a person who, as a result of child abuse, molestation, or sexual abuse, experienced a massive failure in adult life to cope with life stresses and, as a result, entered into conflict with the legal system which resulted in institutionalization (Miller and Veltkemp, 1989b, p. 120).

11

Sexual Boundary Crossings and Violations Between Patient and Therapist

INTRODUCTION

Sexual boundary violations have become an important focus in understanding the spectrum of abuse and a serious concern for the mental health profession (Brodsky, 1989; Gabbard, 1991; Olante, 1991). Within the construct of sexual boundary violations are intrafamily incest, therapist and patient relationships, and issues related to sexual harassment. This chapter will focus on the relationship between the therapist and the patient.

In 1989, the AMA reinforced the Hippocratic Oath with a specific rule stating "sexual contact between a physician and a patient is unethical because it violates the trust necessary in a physician–patient relationship" (AMA, 1991).

During the 1980s and 1990s, the major health organizations passed ethical rules prohibiting therapist–patient sexual contact (e.g.,

American Psychiatric Association, 1985; American Psychoanalytic Association, 1993).

Although all major mental health organizations prohibit sexual contact in psychotherapeutic relationships, a significant number of therapists continue to engage in sexual or sexualized contact with their patients. Some self-reporting surveys reveal that 3 to 12 percent of therapists have engaged in sexual relationships with at least one patient (Schoener, Milgram, Gonsiorek, Luepker, and Conroe, 1989). One study found 80 percent of therapists who reported any sexual involvement with patients, were sexually intimate with the patient. One study regarding psychiatrists found that 65 percent have counseled at least one patient who has been sexually abused by a previous therapist (Gartrell, Herman, Olante, Feldstein, and Localio, 1987).

Studies indicate that up to 90 percent of patients who engaged in sexual contact with their therapists were psychologically harmed as a result. There is clinical research (Gartrell, Herman, Olante, Feldstein, and Localio, 1987) which argues that the resulting impact and injuries may include sexual dysfunction, anxiety disorder, psychiatric hospitalization, increased risk of suicide, dissociation, depression, internalization, and feelings of guilt, anger, shame, fear, confusion, hatred, and worthlessness (Pope, 1986). In addition, the abuse by the therapist may exacerbate the patient's presenting illness. It may create new psychopathology, such as posttraumatic stress disorder (PTSD; Jorgenson, 1994). Among other issues, patients are vulnerable when they enter treatment. There is a significant power imbalance, that is, the therapist has power over the patient. Often, patients lack self-esteem and are fearful. Sexual contact with clients constitutes misuse of the therapist's power and places the patient in a vulnerable-helpless position.

PREVALENCE DATA

Prevalence data related to sexual boundary violations are vague. Much of the data are derived from questionnaire surveys requesting respondents to be honest and truthful about unethical behavior. Several national surveys have been completed suggesting prevalence in the range of 12 percent among male therapists and 3 percent among female therapists (Kluft, 1990). The study, which surveyed three major mental health professions, psychiatry, clinical psychology, and clinical social work, found no differences among the mental health disciplines in the incidence of such sexual boundary violations. The professions have also made considerable efforts to understand the origins and processes of sexual boundary crossings and violations.

Elliot (1990), addressing the issue of abuse-related countertransference and the therapist as an abuse survivor, suggests that clinicians are even more likely than other professionals to have been sexually or physically abused and to have come from homes where substance abuse was a problem for parents. Unresolved child abuse issues can impede or interfere with therapeutic effectiveness with patients. Sexual boundary violations are, perhaps, the most dangerous form of abuse-related countertransference. Boundary incursion by a person entrusted to be a therapeutic agent may not only revisit and restimulate the abuse-related issues for the patient, but reinforce abuse-related trauma in the survivor-client. Megana (1990), researching this area, has concluded that sexual abuse survivors who are sexually revictimized by their therapists suffer greater symptomatology than cohorts who were molested as children but not during therapy.

Gabbard (1991) addressed the psychodynamics of such violations wherein therapists who transgressed sexual boundaries with patients show considerable confusion of their own needs with the patient's needs, or experience a sense of love-sickness or psychopathic exploitation. Most notable among these psychodynamic themes are:

1. Confusion of one's own need to be loved with those of the patient, particularly when one is vulnerable due to personal problems.
2. The fantasy that love in and of itself may be curative.
3. The proneness of the therapist–patient dyad to reenact incestuous sexual involvement from the patient's past.
4. The close linkage between therapeutic zeal and sexual involvement.
5. The tendency of some psychotherapists to act out their hostility at their profession or mentors through sexual exploitation of the patient. In addition, the therapist may sexually exploit a patient simply because he or she wants to or because the opportunity presents itself.

Whether in intrafamily incest, sexual boundary violations in the therapist–patient relationship, or in the medium of sexual harassment, three main methodologies have been utilized to collect data on the characteristics of the perpetrator. Olante (1991) identifies these data summaries as including: (1) composites of the descriptions of such perpetrators based on their treatment; (2) profile descriptions of perpetrators extrapolated from research service surveys that guarantee anonymity to the psychotherapist; (3) a detailed classification and description of offenders based on voluntary evaluations of such offenders by national centers that specialize in the diagnosis and treatment of victims of physical and sexual abuse.

Olante (1991) and Wohlberg (1990) report that characteristics frequently seen include a middle-aged therapist, usually a male, who is undergoing some type of personal distress, who is isolated professionally, who tends to overvalue his or her healing capacity, is unorthodox about his therapeutic methods, frequently personalizes the therapeutic relationship, and who ignores or denies his ethical responsibility to his patients.

WARNING SIGNS OR INDICATIONS OF SEXUALLY INAPPROPRIATE BEHAVIOR

In some cases of sexual exploitation or sexual abuse, the client or patient will notice that a precursor to these behaviors may involve sexually suggestive or other inappropriate behaviors. Often these behaviors are confusing and subtle and can be identified by the client/patient because they often feel uncomfortable. Examples of warning signs include: (1) telling sexually tainted jokes or stories; (2) giving the client or patient seductive looks; (3) discussions of the therapist's sex life or details regarding intimate relationships; (4) sitting too close to the client or patient, kissing or inappropriate touching.

In addition, other warning signals present include: (1) a therapist giving a client special status by scheduling after-hours appointments; (2) charging lower than usual fees; (3) making out-of-office appointments; (4) using the client as a confidant or for personal support; (5)

giving or accepting major gifts; (6) borrowing money; (7) getting involved in business deals with a client; (8) offering alcohol or drugs during therapy.

IMPACT OF VICTIMIZATION

The impacts of victimization can be short or long term depending on a number of factors including: (1) the duration of the abuse or exploitation; (2) whether there was a use of threat or intimidation within the context of the abusive behavior; and (3) the degree to which the abusive behavior occurred. However, even the most minimal forms of sexual exploitation can cause substantial psychological damage to patients. For example, many victims will (1) feel a sense of shame; (2) feel guilty even though it is the therapist's responsibility to keep sexual behavior out of the therapy; (3) have mixed feelings toward the therapist, for example, betrayal, love, anger, or feeling protective; (4) feeling isolated and empty; (5) feeling unable to trust their own feelings or to judge trustworthiness in other people; (6) fear that no one will believe them or understand what has happened or fear that others will find out; (7) posttraumatic stress related symptoms including unexpressed rage, numbness, nightmares, obsessive thoughts, depression, suicidal thoughts, or flashbacks; (8) confusion about dependency, control, power.

PERPETRATOR/VICTIM PROFILES

Composites of perpetrators which emerge include impaired reality testing and poor social judgment, sociopathy and narcissism, ignorance and naiveté, neuroses, and impulsiveness.

Schoener et al. (1989) have identified psychiatric data received in the voluntary evaluation of offenders. They classified sexually exploitative therapists into clusters, based on their years of clinical experience, rather than through systematic research. Their categories include:

1. Uninformed naive—Those individuals who lack knowledge of the expected ethical standards or lack understanding of professional boundaries and confuse personal and professional relationships.
2. Healthy or mildly neurotic—They know the professional standards, actual contact with patients tends to be limited or isolated, situational stressors foster a slow erosion of professional boundaries, the therapists often show remorse.
3. Severely neurotic and socially isolated—These therapists have long-standing emotional problems such as low self-esteem, depression, feelings of inadequacy, and social isolation.
4. Impulsive character disorder—These therapists have long-standing problems with impulse control in many areas of their life, their judgment is poor, and they tend to abuse more than one victim.
5. Sociopathic or narcissistic character disorder—Long-standing serious personal pathology that expresses itself in most aspects of their lives. They manipulate victims and colleagues to protect themselves from their unethical behavior.
6. Psychotic or borderline personality—Impaired reality testing and poor social judgment hinder their ability to apply their knowledge of ethical standards or a clinical understanding of professional boundaries.

Schoener et al. (1989) believe that the uninformed naive and the mildly neurotic have a good prognosis, while the last four have a poor prognosis.

In searching for a victim profile, we must realize that the clinician bears the burden of responsibility for his or her behavior, including ethical and legal considerations, a moral code, and constraints. After an extensive literature review, Wohlberg (1990) has suggested that there is little support for a single profile for patients involved in sexual boundary violations. Gender and age combinations provide a range of diagnostic categories for both parties. What does emerge are "commonalities" representing recurring themes encountered in working with both perpetrators and victims. The central commonality is the vulnerability factor noted in the victim and the clinician.

Stone (1980), examining the issue of vulnerability to sexual exploitation and sexual boundary violations, examined a sample of 46 females who had terminated with male therapists and who were divided into four groups. The groups included those who were sexually intimate, those who were sexually propositioned, prematurely terminated, and those who successfully completed therapy. The study found that women who had been sexually involved with therapists had the strongest anxious attachment to significant others, while there were no significant differences realized between groups and the amount of ego strength.

DSM-IV AND DIAGNOSTIC IMPLICATIONS

As noted in DSM-IV criteria (American Psychiatric Association, 1994a), individuals sexually abused by therapists may have transient stress-related paranoid ideation, expressed inappropriately, and intense anger, affective instability due to marked reactivity of mood, impulsivity in the areas of sex, spending, substance abuse, identity disturbance, and unstable self-image, associations with feelings of imagined abandonment, and a general pattern of unstable interpersonal relationships with alternating extremes of idealization and devaluation. Individuals who may have borderline features, tend to show a pattern of undermining themselves at the moment a goal might be realized. One must realize that the most common pattern in the course of developing the borderline personality is instability in early adulthood, with episodes of affective, impulsive variability. The impairment of the disorder and the risk of self-defeating types of behavior appear to be greatest among young adults.

Borderline personality disorder features are often present. These features generally demonstrate a pattern of instability in interpersonal relationships, poor self-image, impulsivity, and some of the following features:

- Identity disturbance often marked by unstable self-concept or sense of self.
- A pattern of unstable and intense interpersonal relationships that are often marked by alternating extremes of devaluation and idealization.

- Impulsive behavior that tends to be potentially self-damaging and may include self-mutilating behavior and recurrent gestures of suicidal ideation and intent.
- Unstable affective mood and chronic feelings of emptiness.
- Inappropriate and intense anger and poor management of anger and resulting behavior.
- Stress related paranoid ideation with frantic efforts to avoid real or imagined loss or abandonment.

Numerous authors have indicated a history of abuse in the life of these individuals, which may include previous sexual abuse. Herman (1992) has suggested that abused patients learn seductive behavior as a medium by which they relate and reinforce the relationship with the abusing object. Similarly, other clinician researchers (Miller and Veltkamp, 1993) have noted that individuals who experience abuse in childhood may be more likely to enter abusive situations in adulthood, suggesting their need for high-intensity emotional responsivity.

There may also be a model which suggests the presence of borderline personality and a history of abuse as comorbid factors. Herman (1992) suggests that patients diagnosed as borderline may have also been sexually abused, and that this event may indeed play a critical causative role in the formation of symptoms and the vulnerability factor noted in sexual boundary violations. It appears that where there was incestuous sexual abuse in childhood by father or brother, the therapist may repeat that role for the victim. The dynamic of repetition compulsion is seen as critically important to understanding the dynamics of the sexual boundary violation from the victim's perspective.

TREATMENT ISSUES AND IMPLICATIONS

Therapeutic response and intervention to the issues related to sexual boundary violations require various approaches to treatment of both the victim and the perpetrator. The most important therapeutic guidelines include:

1. Recognizing and interrupting sexual boundary violations;

2. Identifying areas of potential risk in the clinical aspects of the patient–therapist relationship;
3. Identifying specific means of evaluating the severity and impact on both perpetrator and victim;
4. The designing of programs to reduce risk in clinical aspects of patient care;
5. Establishing and maintaining operational linkages which address the needs of both patient and therapist in the therapeutic relationship;
6. Preparing reports of incidents as required by statute, and submitting appropriate reports to the Department of Health and the Environment and other appropriate licensing agencies, as mandated by law.
7. Establishing treatment programs for perpetrators and victims.

In assessing the issue of outcome, the prognosis is more favorable if the offender (1) recognizes the problem; (2) takes responsibility for the problem; (3) is willing to go for treatment; and (4) remains in treatment until behavior changes occur. Good intentions are not sufficient.

The prognosis is less than favorable if the offender: (1) does not see the problem; (2) refuses to take full responsibility; (3) is not willing to go for treatment; (4) uses denial and/or projection.

WHAT THE VICTIM CAN DO

A victim may be confused and feel overwhelmed in attempting to decide what to do or whom to tell. The following guidelines should be helpful:

1. Facing what has happened is usually painful, but it is the first step in healing and recovering from the experience.
2. It is important for victims to realize that it does not matter if they wanted the sexual involvement with the therapist; it is the therapist's responsibility never to use the therapy relationship for his or her own sexual gain.
3. The victim should get help from a rape crisis center or any therapist with a sensitivity toward this type of problem.

4. Self-education about therapist abuse can help. One good resource is *Couched in Silence: An Advocacy Handbook on Sexual Exploitation in Therapy* (Consumers Against Sexual Exploitation, 5036 North 56th St., Milwaukee, WI 53218).
5. Many victims want to get information on whether or not their therapist's behavior has been unethical or illegal. This may be accomplished by contacting state licensing boards, rape crisis centers, or the ethical standard committees of state and national professional organizations.

GUIDELINES FOR SANCTIONS

It is recommended that licensure boards have as their highest priority protection of the consumer, although rehabilitation of the offending professional is also important. In many states, sexual misconduct with clients or patients is considered a sex crime. Therefore, it may be appropriate for the board to remove the offending professional's license for an indefinite period. In other cases, it may be appropriate to suspend the license for specific periods of time along with specific recommendations for supervision of the professional's practice and therapy. In some cases, limited practice options may be more appropriate and may include limiting the practice of the professional: (1) by compelling the professional to practice in a different setting; (2) changing the client, patient, or student mix; or (3) changing the degree of independence in the practice through supervision or some other means (Jordan and Walker, 1995).

Multiple solutions have been proposed. The therapist could be moved to a setting which offers less opportunity for individual contact with patients or changed from clinical to administrative responsibilities. The professional may have his or her future practice limited to members of a certain sex, depending on sexual orientation, theoretically to remove temptation. The professional might be limited to practicing with populations which are less vulnerable to the professional's particular interests or familiarities. Finally, the professional may be required to practice in an area where there is clear supervision.

If the latter solution is chosen, the selection of the supervisor is important and must be one who takes the offense seriously, has a full appreciation for boundary problems, and understands the ramifications in clinical practice. In addition, the supervisory process should include the professional being placed under the supervision of the board-appointed supervisor. The board may consider notifying the professional's clients or patients of the action that the board had taken and that a supervisor had been appointed.

Clark and Walker (1995) have identified a number of warning signals of potential boundary crossings or violations. These include the following:

1. Strong feelings about the client;
2. Overextending sessions;
3. Offering transportation to the client;
4. Therapy on a stroll, taking a walk outside of the therapist's office;
5. Off hours calls to and from clients;
6. Gifts;
7. Doing *for* instead of *with* the client;
8. Loaning the client money;
9. Eating meals with the client;
10. Self-disclosures;
11. Support, most touch, and all sex.

FREQUENTLY ASKED QUESTIONS THERAPISTS SHOULD KNOW REGARDING SEXUAL BOUNDARY VIOLATIONS*

Q: Is it normal to feel attracted to your therapist?

A: Yes, it is normal to feel attracted to someone who is attentive, kind, and caring. This is an understandable reaction towards someone helpful to you. However, ethical therapy does not include sex with clients. It is the therapist's responsibility to maintain a relationship that is beneficial to the client.

Q: What if I was the one who brought up having sex?

---

*From: Kentucky Society of Clinical Social Work; *Safety in Therapy: Guidelines for Clinicians* (1996)

A: That doesn't matter. The therapist is solely responsible for keeping sexual exploitation out of therapy.

Q: Am I a victim if I had sex with my therapist?

A: Yes.

Q: What if I try another therapist and he or she blames me for the sexual relationship with my last therapist?

A: Go to another therapist.

Q: Does this kind of unethical behavior happen a lot?

A: A recent study revealed probably less than 10 percent of all therapists have had sexual contact with their clients. However, 80 percent of the sexually exploiting therapists have exploited more than one client; that is, if a therapist is exploiting one client, odds are he will exploit others as well.

Q: Why do some therapists sexually exploit their clients?

A: There may be as many answers to this as there are exploitative therapists. It's important to understand that even if the therapist is experiencing a personal crisis or an attraction to the client, this does not justify or explain the misconduct.

Q: Why do I feel scared or confused about reporting the therapist to the authorities?

A: Feelings of confusion, protectiveness, mutual attraction, shame and guilt are especially common in this type of situation. However, it is important for you to get as much information as possible about your options. Keep in mind you are in control and know what to do.

Q: What if we both feel that we are falling in love and discontinue therapy so that we can have a sexual relationship?

A: No. Stopping therapy to have a relationship is not a good idea. If you and your therapist want to have a sexual relationship, you need to change therapists. The therapist needs to seek supervision, or consult with a therapist about resolving his or her issues. Sexual contact between you and the therapist is harmful.

12

Dimensions of Adult Abuse: The Role of the Health Care Provider

INTRODUCTION

Health care providers have developed an increased sensitivity to the recognition and management of family violence. Examined herein are clinical data which enhance the provider's assessment of abuse with specific criteria useful in the diagnosis and referral of abuse victims. Discussed are psychological factors involved in the adaption process and the long-term effects of victimization.

Victimization through adult abuse has been the focus of public concern, clinical recognition, and considerable recent research (Walker, 1992; Miller and Veltkamp, 1993). The impact of abuse is clear both to the victim and those significant others who realize that a change has taken place in the individual's functioning. Allied health care professionals are among the group of health care providers who have developed an increased awareness and sensitivity to the recognition, management, and referral of domestic violence cases. They clearly recognize the profound impact spouse abuse and child abuse can have on the functioning of the family and the resultant depressive features often seen in victims. In addition, allied health professionals are seen as critically important in the multidisciplinary approaches to treatment and are dedicated to helping individuals gain the highest possible degree of functional independence in daily life (McFarland and Waterman, 1988).

Some of the most significant characteristics of at-risk individuals are people who: (1) have a history of family violence, abuse, or neglect; (2) have disorganized and dysfunctional families; (3) have families who lack interest in or do not accept the victim; and (4) have families that communicate poorly.

The allied health provider, in assessing the presence of adult abuse, needs to be sensitive to the symptoms and indicators that may likely identify the presence of physical, emotional, or psychological abuse. Furthermore, there may be a constellation of factors that should be easily recognized by allied health care providers. These include, but are not limited to:

1. Is one partner, more than the other, very passive, dependent, and reluctant to assert themselves for fear of destroying the family unit?
2. Is there a constrictiveness in the communication and poor interpersonal relationship between the spouses, perhaps reflecting marital discord?
3. How does the patient process stress, anxiety, tension, within the family?
4. Are there adequate coping skills, particularly under stress?
5. Is there little or no social contact for the patient outside the family network?

Within the framework of adult abuse, it is not uncommon that the family will remain closed until another person recognizes some of the signs and symptoms of family violence and gently begins to explore this in more detail.

The trauma involved in adult abuse is often difficult to understand. There is usually extreme difficulty in discussing any aspects of the victimization. The victim confronted with such abuse often passes through a series of stages that deal with various aspects of the trauma. Walker (1996) suggests a cycle theory of violence which includes a tension-building phase, an acute battering phase, and a honeymoon phase. As tension rises in the relationship, the anger and rage for the perpetrator is physically projected onto the victim through beating or battering or emotional abuse. Following the incidence, the honeymoon phase occurs for the victim and the perpetrator wherein the victim often reinforces the hope that the relationship will improve.

The Trauma Accommodation Syndrome (Miller and Veltkamp, 1989b) argues that the victim processes the trauma of abuse by moving through a series of stages or phases. The initial stage of the victimization is recognized as the *stressor,* usually realizing an acute physical or psychological trauma. The person's response is usually one of feeling overwhelmed and intimidated. The locus of control is more of an external nature. It is, therefore, not uncommon for the victim to think recurringly of this stressful life experience and to focus on the intimidating factors in the abuse itself.

The acute stage of traumatization is followed by a stage which involves *cognitive disorganization,* confusion, grieving, and helplessness. This stage is marked by vagueness in understanding both the concept of abuse and expectancies associated with the demand of the perpetrator.

The third stage involves *avoidance,* which can either be a conscious inhibition, where an effort is made on the part of the victim to actively inhibit the thoughts and feelings related to the domestic violence and traumatization, or it can involve outward avoidance involving unconscious denial that the victimization is occurring. The perpetrator often feeds into the cycle of abuse and reinforces the desire to impair the relationship. Men who abuse are victimized by their own lack of communication skills, fear of intimacy, and dependency on the women they batter. The society in which we live encourages men to be action-oriented, be problem solvers, and to suppress feelings. Often recognized characteristics of a batterer include low self-esteem, a traditional view of the role of men and women in society, and the blaming of others for the actions that result in the domestic violence.

THE ROLE OF THE HEALTH CARE PROVIDER IN DOMESTIC VIOLENCE

Within the scope of mental health services, allied health care staff can benefit children, adolescents, adults, and the elderly who may be victimized in some way through various forms of domestic violence (Table 11.1 summarizes key indicators of abuse). Numerous clinical programs are dedicated to helping individuals gain the highest potential of functional independence, and by being alert to the signs and symptoms of domestic violence, may serve an important role in the recognition that various forms of abuse may be occurring. DeJong (1985) suggests the following objectives be addressed in the recognition and treatment of victims of abuse:

1. Identify who is a victim or victims of abuse and who is the abuser. Some victims will complain directly about assaults, while others exhibit various physical and vague symptoms.
2. Manage the acute medical problems first by referring appropriately to physicians and other health care professionals available to deal with the problems themselves.
3. Obtain and record accurate histories of the assault, including the answers to the questions of who, when, where, what, and how.
4. Manage the acute emotional problems that are usually experienced by the victims through appropriate referral to mental health services. Oftentimes there are mixed feelings of anger, frustration, and guilt.
5. Safeguard the victim against further abuse by assisting in the determination as to whether the patient, child, adult, or elderly person should be returned to a home situation or be placed in temporary custody.
6. Aid in the formulation of a treatment plan and follow-up plans for the victim's medical and psychological needs.
7. Comply with legal requirements for the collection of evidence, documentation, and depending on the laws of a particular state, reporting the abuse as a crime.

Objectives such as these are best achieved through multidisciplinary efforts that involve specially trained individuals, including effective interface between physicians and allied health providers, working together with the legal system with the child and adult protective service agencies in addressing the issues of adult abuse.

Table 11.1 *Physical, Behavioral, and Psychological Indicators of Adult Abuse*

Physical Indicators:

1. Unexplained bruises and welts on the face, lips, mouth, torso, back, buttocks
2. Unexplained fractures to skull, nose, or facial structure; in various stages of healing, multiple or spiral fractures
3. Injury often in body areas covered by clothing or hair
4. Explanation for injury doesn't fit

Behavioral Indicators:

1. Emotional constriction or blunted affect
2. Extreme withdrawal or aggressiveness
3. Apprehension, fearfulness
4. Depressive features

Psychological Indicators:

1. Irritability, restlessness
2. Sleep disturbances—insomnia, nightmares, etc.
3. Difficulty concentrating
4. Exaggerated started response
5. Apprehension, anticipatory anxiety
6. Phobias, obsessions
7. Depression
8. Anger
9. Anxiety
10. Phobias

RECOGNITION, DOCUMENTATION, NOTIFICATION, AND REFERRAL

The role and function of the providers in the recognition and referral of the victims of adult abuse is critically important (Select Committee on Aging, 1980, 1981). Therapists are often part of the network of health care professionals who have the opportunity to identify abuse when they are assessing the health care of victims. The therapist experienced in detecting physical, psychological, and behavioral indicators of potential abuse can evaluate further the need for services and appropriately refer to the multidisciplinary team. The allied health care providers can be instrumental in the recognition and referral of victims of domestic violence and adult abuse and should document, notify, and intervene using guidelines summarized in Table 11.2.

Table 11.2 *Documentation Notification and Intervention Procedures in Assessing and Reporting Abuse*

Identification History & findings	Notification
Victim report	Report orally or in writing to appropriate county office and Cabinet for Human Resources
Pattern of physician hopping	
Previous unexplained injuries	
Previous reports of similar injuries	
Unexplained delay in seeking treatment	Include in written report:
Series of missed medical appointments	Name, address, age of person, and anyone responsible for his or her care
Patient appears fearful of companion	
Conflicting accounts of incident by patient and companion	
Absence of assistance, attitudes of indifference or toward patient by companion	Nature and extent of abuse, neglect, or exploitation
Companion denies patient a chance to interact	Identity of perpetrator
	Any other helpful information
Intervention	
Consent for treatment	
Consent for treatment is obtained via application for care	
Treat physical and medical injuries and provide counseling and referral through appropriate community agencies with follow-up services until safety and resolution is realized.	

COMMUNITY RESOURCES

There are numerous community resources available for information and referral. For the health care professional who recognizes potential signs and symptoms of domestic violence, such referrals may be of benefit in aiding the individual who has been victimized. These resources include:

1. Reporting: Most states require immediate reporting of any suspicion of abuse to adult protective services.
2. Counseling and casework services: These services are often designed to facilitate the victim's exploration of alternatives and eventual return to the community.
3. Safe shelters and 24-hour crisis hotlines: Services such as these provide a place where victims and abusers can call anytime, day or night, to receive counseling, information, referrals, and screening for shelter placement.
4. Legal advocacy programs: Services such as these provide a legal advocate to act as a liaison between the victims of domestic violence and their perpetrators, whether residing at a shelter or through the court system.
5. Hospital advocacy programs: Services such as these provide information, support, and referral.
6. Community education: Services such as these provide programs on issues of domestic violence for public awareness.

13

Legal Considerations in Recognizing Adult Victimization

Judith Sheiman, Ph.D., J.D.

INTRODUCTION

A litigation oriented society has heightened our awareness of the legal aspects of our relationship with clients and our compliance with the legal system. The clinician–client relationship is closed with confidentiality, privacy, and trust. Within the realm of family violence and the spectrum of abuse and neglect are a multiplicity of issues that must be addressed in both the diagnosis and treatment of victims of abuse.

Legal considerations in the recognition, diagnosis, and treatment of the broad area of adult abuse and its impact on the lives of both victims and perpetrators have gained considerable attention in our society (Summit, 1983; Miller and Veltkamp, 1989a; Walker, 1992). Maltreated and abused individuals have been the focus of public concern, clinical assessment, and treatment. Epidemiological studies (Conte, Berlinger and Schuerlan, 1987; National Center for Child Abuse and Neglect, 1988) have provided convincing evidence that abuse may well be occurring at alarmingly higher rates than earlier realized.

DUTY TO REPORT ABUSE

Since 1988, all of the United States has had some type of elder abuse legislation and the majority of states include a requirement to report abuse (Vandecreek and Knapp, 1993). In most states, the law applies to adults who are dependent on others because they are physically or mentally unable to care for themselves. The target populations usually include the elderly and the disabled. The statutes are similar to the child abuse reporting statutes but often include financial exploitation as well as physical abuse and neglect. If a clinician has a reasonable suspicion that abuse, neglect, or exploitation has occurred he or she must report it to the appropriate agency, typically the department of social services or a local law enforcement agency.

In the case of adult abuse, abuse or neglect usually means the infliction of physical pain, injury, or mental injury or the deprivation of services by a caregiver that are necessary to maintain the health and welfare of the adult. In some states, e.g., Kentucky, the statute is broad and includes any abuse against an adult. Cases of domestic violence are included as reportable. Death of the adult does not release the clinician from the duty to report.

While research is still divided as to whether there are clear risk factors in elder abuse, certain characteristics should raise red flags for clinicians (Kapp, 1995). Elderly people who are extremely dependent on others because of extreme financial, physical, or mental hardship may particularly be at risk. Social isolation and poor financial resources also increase the possibility of abuse occurring.

A report to another agency of abuse or neglect should be done immediately upon discovering the reportable behavior. While a telephone call can be sufficient for the initial report, it is probably best that the clinician follow up the call with a written letter, sent return receipt requested. This ensures that there is a paper trail showing that the abuse was reported to the proper agency. The clinician should include all information available, including name and address of the victim and perpetrator, nature and extent of the abuse, neglect, or exploitation, including any evidence of previous abuse, neglect, or exploitation, and any other useful information. It is extremely important that clinicians find out the laws of their State pertaining to this issue and act accordingly.

DUTY TO WARN

The 1976 California Supreme Court decision in Tarasoff v. Regents of University of California stated that psychotherapists have a duty to protect potential victims from dangerous clients. Since that time, many state courts have decided similar cases and come to similar conclusions. This duty is based on the special relationship between therapist and client. A therapist is considered to have accepted responsibility for the behavior of the client when he or she accepted the client for treatment. The Tarasoff case found that the duty applied even though the victim had not specifically been identified. The Court pointed out that the victim was readily identifiable as Tarasoff. The therapist in the case tried to have the client committed, but after talking to him the police decided the client did not need to be committed. The Court said that this was not enough, the duty to warn required the therapist to take one or more of various possible steps. These included warning the victim, instituting commitment procedures, or telling the police. The Court decided that doing the latter two was not sufficient and that the therapist should also have warned the intended victim.

The responsibility is not absolute, a therapist is not responsible for what he or she does not know nor for when he or she has used reasonable care. The Court said the most important factor was ''foreseeability'' (Tarasoff v. Regents of University of California, 1976). They rejected the argument of the American Psychiatric Association and other professional societies that the reliability of dangerousness prediction is low. The Court stated that the prediction did not have to be definitive, just reasonable. How this case is applied to future individual cases has been a source of conflict ever since.

The court in Jablonski by Pahls v. U.S. (1983) found the therapists liable for failure to warn the wife of a man with a history of dangerousness. The police had told one psychiatrist about some of Jablonski's history of violence but that psychiatrist did not pass the information on to the treating psychiatrist. They did not attempt to get Jablonski's past psychiatric records. The psychiatrist told the victim to leave Jablonski, and her response was that she was in love with him. The psychiatrist decided against further warnings because he did not believe they would be effective. Other psychiatrists at the hospital told the victim and her mother to stay away from Jablonski. Jablonski never made any specific threats nor indicated that he was planning violence. Despite this, the Court found the therapists liable. They said that if the psychiatrists had gotten Jablonski's past records it would have been obvious that he was dangerous and that he was likely to choose his wife as victim. The Court found the warnings given to be inadequate.

Another court expanded the duty to other people, in this case the child of the victim, who were easily identifiable and foreseeable as likely to be near the victim when violence occurs (Hedlund v. Superior Court of Orange City, 1983). The case gave no guidelines as to how to determine whether a relationship fits this category.

Other courts have limited the application of the Tarasoff doctrine. In Thompson v. County of Alameda (1980) the Court found that no duty to warn existed when a client makes "nonspecific threats of harm directed at nonspecific victims." In Brady v. Hopper (1983), James Brady sued John Hinckley's psychiatrist for not warning the President that Hinckley was a danger to him. However, Hinckley had not made threats against a specific person and this court also found that the duty to protect and warn did not include cases where no victim was identified and threats were not specifically made.

CLINICAL PRACTICE AND TARASOFF

Overall, most states have upheld Tarasoff-like cases. Considering the general trend, therapists have been advised to act as though this duty exists (Vandecreek and Knapp, 1993) regardless of whether or not their state has had a similar case. Good practice includes learning techniques to evaluate dangerousness in clients and keeping detailed and comprehensive written records. A simple statement that the client would like to kill someone is probably not enough to constitute reportable violence absent any other factors. The most important thing a clinician can do is to find out what the law is in their state. The state psychology association usually is a good place to find this information.

Evaluations for violence are similar to suicide evaluations. There are several good articles and books about risk assessment, e.g. Monahan (1981). Briefly, therapists need to determine if the client has a plan to commit violence. How well thought-out and realistic the plan is may be important. If the client has a plan, does he intend to and have the means to carry it out? Is there a history of violence? Factors such as depression, social isolation, agitation, impulsivity, and alcohol or drug use will increase the risk of violence.

Therapists should routinely request past therapy records from their clients. This should really be done in all client cases, whether or not the therapist suspects potential for violence. If the client refuses, the request and refusal by the client should be carefully documented. If records are sent for and not received, again, this should be documented. As seen in Jablonski by Pahls v. U.S. (1983), if past records show a history of violence, the therapist may be liable even if the client has never made an actual threat. Again, what is important is what a reasonable therapist should do—if the therapist requests past records and is refused, he or she is not likely to be held liable for not having access to those records.

In the same vein, the therapist is most likely to be found liable when no evaluation was done but not when an evaluation was done, the client lied, and/or the therapist was incorrect. The standard that is used in court is whether a reasonable therapist, with the same abilities, under the conditions and with the knowledge that existed at that time, would have found the client to be a risk and made an intervention.

An important component of determining response to potential violence is consultation with other professionals. Since the standard a therapist is held to is that of reasonable care, evidence that other professionals in the community concur with the action taken is strong evidence that reasonable care was taken. All consultations should be carefully documented.

The warning of a potential victim is only one of the possible required responses to future violence. Clinicians may be required to institute involuntary or voluntary commitment proceedings. The clinician may make changes in therapy, such as seeing the client more frequently, having a contract to do no harm (similar to a contract not to commit suicide), and other appropriate therapeutic interventions. All such interventions should be carefully documented and kept in the client's record.

SUMMARY

In general, everything that is said or done in connection with cases involving violence should be carefully documented. One of the biggest mistakes clinicians' can make is to refuse to document their cases, assuming that if it isn't written down it cannot be brought up in court. Another major error is to attempt to alter or destroy records after a violent episode has occurred. Either of these behaviors creates a strong appearance of guilt. The majority of therapists (making up the hypothetical "reasonable" therapist) do keep written records. Refusal to do so will appear unusual and make it look as though the clinician had something to hide. Similarly, altering or destroying records appears even more suspicious. If it is necessary when making a written note to make changes, a single line should be drawn through the material so that it is still readable although obviously meant to be discarded. This removes the temptation to assume the clinician was trying to hide negative information.

For all these cases, consultation with other professionals is important. Many state psychology associations and malpractice insurers provide consultations with legal experts for their members. In a case where a clinician is uncertain whether or not to report abuse to a Department of Social Services agency, most agencies are willing to give advice. The clinician can describe the case without identifying information and be advised as to whether this is a case that would typically be reported. Again, it is extremely important to fully document all consultations, including the name of the person with whom one consulted.

Considering that these cases often involve breaking confidentiality, it is a good idea to warn clients of these exceptions to the general rule of confidentiality before they begin therapy. Many states have laws that protect therapists' from actions by clients for breaking confidentiality if the therapist did so in good faith and with good reason. However, in order to obtain a truly informed consent to therapy, clients should be made aware of the times that their confidentiality will not be maintained (i.e., child or elder abuse, suicide, violence or, in some states, domestic abuse). Unless clients know the risks of disclosure in therapy, they cannot make a fully informed decision about making those disclosures.

Most of all, clinicians must keep in mind that the law, both statutory and case law, can vary from state to state. One state need not follow the laws of another, although often this is the case. It is important for clinician's to be aware of the laws of their own state that cover these issues.

Afterword

Adult Abuse: Critical Issues for the Decade

Current trends in assessing the impact of adult abuse on the health of individuals have brought to public attention the complexity and multiplicity of factors that must be considered in assessing and treating victims (Figley, 1985; Green, 1990; Friedman, 1991; Dohrenwend, Raphael, Schwartz, Stueve, and Skodol, 1993; Miller and Kraus, 1995; Clark and Miller, 1996).

Within these assembled chapters are critically important topics that focus on the impact of adult abuse from the trauma itself to the symptoms that may result. There emerges a dose–effect relationship in which the risk of the developing psychopathology related to adult abuse increases with intensity and duration of the trauma. A continuum of sorts emerges which includes the components of learning theory, various personality characteristics, and the presence of support systems. The perceived locus of control of victims, and the psychoneuroimmunological aspects of adjustment must be considered.

Several questions have emerged that guide us in our effort to understand the critical issues in adult abuse as a stressful life event. These include:

1. How are adult abuse and its symptoms diagnosed?
2. How do we assess the impact of adult abuse?
3. How do humans process trauma from adult abuse?
4. Is abuse a learned behavior?
5. Is there a "don't blame me" syndrome?
6. Are mandatory reporting laws helpful to victims of abuse?
7. Are there ethnocultural variants of abuse?
8. Which treatment models are most helpful to traumatized persons?
9. What research do practitioners need?
10. What are the prevention–intervention strategies for the decade?

Friedman (1993) has noted that the biological research suggests that patients with posttraumatic stress disorder (PTSD), which is frequently associated with child and adult victimization, display marked abnormalities and sympathetic nervous system arousal and hypothalamic pituitary–adrenal–cortical function in the indigenous opioid system and in the physiology of sleep and dreaming. There is encouragement toward a biopsychosocial model in which many different factors contribute to our understanding of traumatization and stress and the realization that this diagnostic entity is not a single psychiatric disorder, but rather a more complex spectrum disorder.

HOW ARE ADULT ABUSE AND ITS SYMPTOMS DIAGNOSED?

Over the past decade, we have realized that one major impact of abusive experiences on its victims has come to be known as posttraumatic stress disorder (Miller, 1993). More recent inquiry into this question suggests that it may be more important to look at the impact of adult abuse on health as a spectrum disorder rather than as a single disorder in and of itself. In viewing this as a spectrum disorder (Figure 1), we recognize that anxiety and depression are widely present in individuals who have experienced adult abuse.

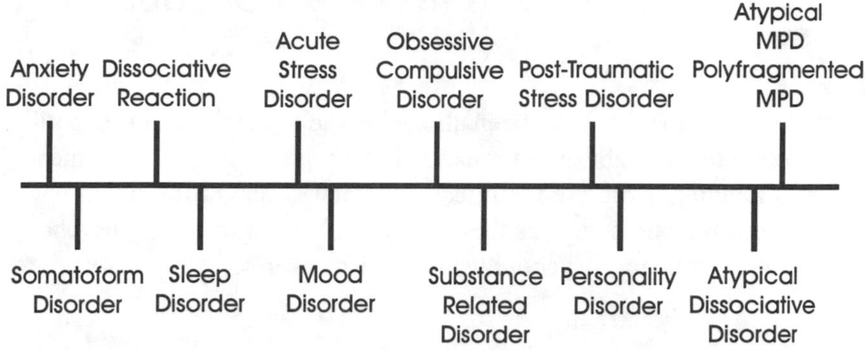

Figure 1. Spectrum Disorder of Abuse

Of importance to the numbing and restricted range of emotional experiences found in traumatized individuals is the role of anger. For many, anger is a frequently expressed emotion that creates multiple interpersonal problems. For some, the control of anger and the accompanying fear of loss of control are major preoccupations that cause considerable distress and frequently lead to social withdrawal and isolation.

The startle response seen in traumatized individuals may be similar to that found in generalized anxiety disorder. The exaggerated startle response may reflect a psychophysiological arousal which is noticeably worsened in the presence of specific situational reminders and triggers.

Finally, the presence of dual diagnosis has been important in understanding the complexity of the impact of trauma on the individual's functioning. The presence of coexisting Axis I or Axis II disorders has considerable clinical revelance in influencing formulation of the patient's problem in both an etiological and treatment perspective. Frequently traumatized individuals can meet the criteria for major depression, substance abuse/dependence, and various components of anxiety disorders, including panic disorder. The identification of coexisting disorders at the onset of treatment can influence decision making regarding the sequence and timing of specific interventions and strategies that can be potentially helpful in optimizing treatment outcome.

HOW DO WE ASSESS THE IMPACT OF ADULT ABUSE?

Numerous approaches have been utilized in the assessment of traumatization due to adult abuse. Summarized in chapter 3 are multiple measures including structured clinical interviews, diagnostic interview scales, and specific measures that have been helpful including psychometric measures and psychophysiological measures.

HOW DO HUMANS PROCESS TRAUMA FROM ADULT ABUSE?

Figley (1985) and others have generated paradigms for assessing the normal and pathological phases of processing trauma. Generally recognized in these paradigms are a series of stages or phases in which the traumatic event is first recognized. These allow the clinician and victim to decipher both the psychological and physical impact of the traumatization. A summary of these theoretical models is summarized in chapter 2 of this volume. Miller and Veltkamp (1989a, 1993) suggest that the victim processes the trauma by moving through a series of stages and have adapted their model to current criteria consistent with diagnostic indicators. Much can be learned from the work of Summit (1983) and his sexual abuse accommodation syndrome. This model recognizes that a fundamental characteristic of abuse is usually that of silence or secrecy by the victim. In most cases, the victim fails to voice spontaneous and immediate complaint, which can jeopardize the credibility of any later protest and burden the victim with a lifelong sense of being trapped in guilt and complicity. The secrecy paralyzes the individual and becomes so central to the victim's survival that it may trigger elaborate behavioral and mental efforts to conceal the abuse. Summit further argues that the secrecy leads to a state of helplessness, recognizing the immense vulnerability of the victim, who is both speechless and powerless to explain the abuse. This results in a feeling of entrapment and accommodation, a level of acceptance and invitation for the cycle of violence to recur (Walker, 1994).

IS ABUSE A LEARNED BEHAVIOR?

It is recognized that there is no single cause-and-effect relationship between an abusive family relationship and interpersonal violence. Over the past several decades, research has documented that violence in the media is one of the ways a culture teaches violence. When violence and aggression are combined in the media, the message of violence can be translated into abusive types of behavior. Psychological research has demonstrated that it is more effective to reinforce positive behavior than to punish negative behavior. This has been confirmed through studies that demonstrate that there are more negative than positive behaviors acted out in dysfunctional families and behaviors such as these occur in clustered patterns, expressed by both males and females in abusive relationships. Thus, the process by which abuse is learned is circular in form. It begins in the family, expanding through the culture of a larger society in which numerous medians and models of behavior are reinforced and results in a pattern of learned behavior.

IS THERE A "DON'T BLAME ME" SYNDROME?

Allen Dershowitz, in his book entitled *The Abuse Excuse* (1995), has raised a critically important question in the area of abuse in our society. What is the responsibility of an individual for his or her own behavior? When does the use of abuse as a defense become an excuse? Have we created a victim culture which appears to be much more supportive to remaining a victim rather than healing through acceptance of responsibility for behavior? The classic cases which emerge involve adults who have been abused, suffered many consequences, and subsequently brought harm to others. There appears to be a relationship between the absence of resolution of being a victim and displacing or projecting that victimization onto others. The "don't blame me" syndrome must be reexamined and an alternative model developed which argues that victims should be expected to take individual responsibility in addressing their abusive situations. The communities in which we live must commit themselves to stopping violence, improving sensitivity to victims, and providing a medium by which victims emerge from the victim state and do not accommodate victimization into the life-style.

ARE MANDATORY REPORTING LAWS HELPFUL TO VICTIMS OF ABUSE?

The effectiveness of mandatory reporting laws must be examined within the context of addressing adult victimization through abusive situations. What is clear is that many individuals question whether mandatory reporting laws have helped abuse victims and whether existing adult protection and intervention systems have been as helpful as hoped by the judicial and social service system. Adult abuse victims may not receive individual psychotherapy and treatment for the preponderance of symptoms which reveal their traumatization. While treatment plans are often ordered through court proceedings, rarely is access to psychotherapy and other treatment provided in the most effective ways.

ARE THERE ETHNOCULTURAL VARIANTS?

Cross-cultural aspects of adult abuse are of significant importance in understanding the etiology, processing, and adaptation of individuals to the disorder. Cross-cultural studies offer an opportunity to compare like populations who have experienced like stressors with the search for social and cultural correlates that may provide clues to the etiology of certain conditions, their onset, their maintenance, and their resolution.

Boehnlein and Kinzie (1995) note that the diagnosis of psychiatric disorders cross-culturally remains an area of great opportunity and controversy and that traumatization and stress must be analyzed and assessed cross-culturally. Westermeyer (1987) has noted that diagnosis cross-culturally can have a variety of meanings, and raises the question as to whether the clinician from one culture can make a diagnosis for a patient from another culture. It becomes imperative that clinicians and researchers realize that understanding the entire sociocultural milieu in which the patient functions is a critical factor in recognizing diagnostic symptoms consistent with traumatization and stress.

WHICH TREATMENT MODELS ARE MOST HELPFUL TO TRAUMATIZED PERSONS?

There is considerable interest today in understanding the impact of treatment for adult abuse (Walker, 1996). What is being realized, however, is that data from a number of studies have shown that various stressors can adversely affect immune function. The bodily immune system is a complex surveillance apparatus that functions to determine self from nonself. An immune reaction is activated in response to exposure to foreign antigens in an effort to maintain the body's homeostatis. There is ample evidence from human and animal studies that demonstrate the downward modulation of immune function concomitant with stressful life experiences. As a consequence of this, the possible enhancement of immune function by behavioral strategies has generated considerable interest. Clinicians and researchers have used a number of diverse strategies to modulate immune functioning including relaxation, hypnosis, exercise, classical conditioning and exposure to phobic stressors, to enhance perceived coping and self-efficacy through cognitive behavioral interventions.

Prominent among the current therapies used in trauma treatment are psychoanalytic and object relations therapy, psychodynamic, existential and humanistic therapies, cognitive–behavioral and social learning therapies, family therapy and feminist therapy (Worell and Remer, 1992). Detailed discussion of long-term therapeutic interventions has been addressed and discussed elsewhere (Walker, 1994).

Similarly, there are a selected group of traditional therapeutic techniques that have been useful in working with victims of abuse who have developed symptomatology consistent with PTSD. These models of treatment have included hypnosis, symptomatic desynthesization, relaxation therapy, guided imagery, reframing and cognitive restructuring, and eye movement desensitization and reprocessing. The most recent of these therapies has included eye movement desensitization, and reprocessing (Shapiro, 1995) which suggest a behavioral model used in conjunction with relaxation exercises for patients who have experienced trauma that is experienced on an affective rather than a cognitive level.

Finally, survivor therapy (Walker, 1994) is a treatment approach that is designed to provide an intervention based both on feminist therapy theory and trauma theory. Survivor therapy integrates the philosophies of both. The key principles of survivor therapy according to Walker (1994) include:

- Safety and powerment validation
- Emphasis on strengths
- Education
- Expanding alternatives
- Restoring clarity in judgement
- Understanding oppression
- Making one's own decisions

The goal of survivor therapy include: (1) safety; (2) reimprovement; (3) validation; (4) exploring one's options; (5) cognitive clarity in judgment; (6) making one's own decisions; and (7) feeling the effects of trauma. This therapeutic approach argues that excess psychic energy becomes blocked by the traumatization and abuse, and that integration of various developmental issues in the life cycle aids in the process of adaptation and trauma accommodation (Miller and Veltkamp, 1989b).

Appendix A

Model Policy for Reporting Abuse to Responsible Authorities

POLICY:

A. It shall be the policy of ______(name of organization)______ ______________________to comply in principle with the state reporting statutes which serve to protect ______(name)______ ______________________the citizens of ____(county and state)____. Pursuant to this policy, the reporting statutes to be honored shall include:

1. Reporting child abuse
2. Reporting adult abuse
3. Duty of qualified mental health professionals to warn intended victims of patient's threat of violence

B. In accord therefore, with ______________________ Statutes ______ applicable professional codes of ethics, and other federal and state legislation:

1. Duty to report child abuse:

Any person or persons who knows or has reasonable cause to believe that a child is dependent, neglected, or abused, shall immediately cause an oral or written report to be made to a local law enforcement agency, ____________________________ the Department for Social Services or its designated representative, the ______________ Attorney or the County Attorney, by telephone or otherwise.

The oral or written report shall include the following information, if known:

(a) The names and addresses of the child and his or her parents or other persons exercising custodial control or supervision;
(b) The child's age;
(c) The nature and extent of the child's alleged dependency, neglect, or abuse (including any previous charges of dependency, neglect, or abuse) to this child or his/her siblings;
(d) The name and address of the person allegedly responsible for the abuse or neglect;
(e) Any other information that the person making the report believes might be helpful in the furtherance of the purposes of this section.

DEFINITIONS:

"Abused or neglected child" is defined as a child whose health or welfare is harmed or threatened with harm when his parent, guardian, or other person exercising custodial control or supervision of the child: inflicts or allows to be inflicted upon the child, physical or emotional injury by other than accidental means; creates or allows to be created a risk of physical or emotional injury to the child by other than accidental means; commits or allows to be committed an act of sexual abuse, sexual exploitation, or prostitution upon the child; abandons or exploits such child; does not provide the child with adequate care, supervision, food, clothing, shelter and education or medical care necessary for the child's well-being.

"Child" means any person who has not reached his eighteenth (18th) birthday, unless otherwise provided under Kentucky Statutes.

"Dependent child" means any child, other than an abused or neglected child, who is under improper care, custody, control, or guardianship that is not due to an intentional act of the parent, guardian, or person exercising custodial control or supervision of the child.

2. Duty to report adult abuse:

Any person or persons having reasonable cause to suspect that an adult has suffered abuse, neglect, or exploitation, shall immediately cause an oral or written report to be made to a local law enforcement agency, of the ______________________________ the Department for Social Services or its designated representative, the ____________________ or the County Attorney, by telephone or otherwise. Death of an adult does not relieve one of the responsibility for reporting the circumstances surrounding the death.

The oral or written report shall include the following information, if known:

(a) The names and addresses of the adult, or of any other person responsible for his/her care;
(b) The age of the adult;
(c) The nature and extent of the abuse, neglect, or exploitation, including any evidence of previous abuse, neglect, or exploitation;
(d) The identity of the perpetrator, if known;
(e) Any other information that the person making the report believes might be helpful in establishing the cause of the abuse, neglect, or exploitation.

DEFINITIONS:

"Adult" means a person eighteen (18) years of age or older or a married person without regard to age, who because of mental or physical dysfunctioning is unable to manage his or her own resources, carry out the activities of daily living, or protect himself or herself from neglect, hazardous or abusive situations without assistance from others and may be in need of protective services, or who is a victim of abuse or neglect inflicted by a spouse or a cohabiting adult.

"Abuse or neglect" means the infliction of physical pain, injury, or mental injury, or the deprivation of services by a caregiver which are necessary to maintain the health and welfare of an adult, or a situation in which an adult, living alone, is unable to provide or obtain for himself or herself the services which are necessary to maintain his or her health or welfare or a situation in which a person inflicts physical pain or injury upon a spouse or deprives a spouse of reasonable services necessary to maintain the health and welfare of his or her spouse.

3. Duty of Qualified Mental Health Professional to Warn Intended Victim of Patient's Threat of Violence.

The duty to warn or take reasonable precaution to provide protection from violent behavior arises only when the patient has communicated to the qualified mental health professional an actual threat of physical violence against a clearly identified or reasonably identifiable victim, or when the patient has communicated to the qualified mental health professional an actual threat of some specific violent act. The duty to warn a clearly identifiable victim shall be discharged by the qualified mental health professional if reasonable efforts are made:

a. to communicate the threat to the victim, and
b. to notify the police department closest to the patient's and the victim's residence of the threat of violence.

When the patient has communicated to the qualified mental health professional an actual threat of some specific violent act and no particular victim is identifiable, the duty to warn has been discharged if reasonable efforts are made to communicate the threat to law enforcement authorities.

The duty to take reasonable action to provide protection from violent behavior shall be satisfied if reasonable efforts are made to seek civil commitment of the patient.

Appendix B

Model Intake Contact Form for Abuse

Today's Date________	Walk-in________	ID #________
Time________AM	Phone________	SS #________
________PM	Outreach________	Welfare/________
________	Written________	Medicaid #________

SERVICE REQUESTED FOR
Client's NAME ________________________
First Middle Last

Permanent ________
Address ________________________ Temporary ________
Street City/Town Zip County

Catchment Area ________

Phone # ________ Means of Transportation ________
Directions to home (if outreach) ________________

____

Sex ________ Male ________ Date of Birth ________ Age ________
Female ________

SERVICE REQUESTED BY

☐ AGENCY Name__________ Phone #__________

☐ OTHER Address__________ Time(s) seen by__________

☐ SELF If Agency, Contact Person__________ the agency__________

PRESENTING SITUATION/PROBLEM: What made you decide to seek help today?

Type of abuse

Abused verbally/ emotionally/ psychologically

Kicked

Hit with an object

Punched/slapped

Imprisoned

Nonconsensual sex/sexual torture

Multiple forms of physical abuse

Combined physical and sexual abuse

Combined physical-psychological abuse

Comined psychological and sexual abuse

Combined sexual-physical-psychological abuse

Have you talked with anyone about this? Yes ____ Who? __________

Address __________ No ____ Phone # __________

Date of last contact__________

PSYCHIATRIC HISTORY

I. Identifying data
II. Chief complaint
III. History of present illness
IV. Previous illnesses
    A. Psychiatric
    B. Medical
V. Past personal history
    A. Prenatal and perinatal
    B. Early childhood (through age 3)
    C. Middle childhood (ages 3-11)
    D. Late childhood (puberty through adolescence)
    E. Adulthood
        1. Occupational history
        2. Marital and relationship history
        3. Military history
        4. Educational history
        5. Religion
        6. Social activity
        7. Current living situation
    F. Psychosexual history
    G. Family history

Are you taking ANY medication now? Yes ______ What? 1. ________________
No ______ 2. ________________
3. ________________

CRISIS RATING
☐ Immediate
☐ Within a few hours
☐ Within 24 hours

OUTCOME

______RESOLVED
______UNRESOLVED
______RESCHEDULED____________
______REFERRED TO____________
______REFERRED TO COMMUNITY AGENCY

PROVIDER: ________________________

Appendix C

Prevention Strategies in Adult Abuse and Neglect at the Primary, Secondary, and Tertiary Levels

Primary Prevention

1. Projects that focus on family communication
2. Projects that interrupt the cycle of abuse
3. Projects that increase understanding of the abuse process
4. Projects that maximize helping networks for victims and perpetrators

Secondary Prevention

1. Identify persons & communities at risk for abuse & neglect
2. Monitor high risk situations
3. Provide education and therapy for persons who are victims of abuse
4. Sensitize to dual diagnosis situations in abused persons

Tertiary Prevention

1. Reduce the incidence and prevalence of abuse
2. Provide adult protective service programs for victims
3. Assess need for guardianship and placement services
4. Monitor and assure that guardians have the best interests of the patient in mind
5. Maximize services from multiple sources beyond the primary caregiver

Appendix D

Courtroom Testimony: Preparation and Court Behavior

GENERAL CONSIDERATIONS

1. The definition of an expert witness is anyone who has had experience or training in a designated field.
2. It is crucial to have confidence in yourself and your evaluation.
3. Do not increase your fees per unit of time for court work as this makes you vulnerable in the court room. Include all planning, preparation, evaluation, discussion with attorneys, depositions, and testimony in your fee.
4. Evaluate the possibility that parents fake well when dealing with custody or abuse cases, or fake badly, for example, in personal injury cases. It is often helpful to see all family members to help get a more objective view, rather than only interviewing the victim.

5. You will be asked questions regarding your qualifications. Include your professional training, any additional training, licensure, workshops you have given, consultations, academic appointments, professional organizations, all publications and research.

PREPARATION FOR COURT

1. Do not look sloppy or flamboyant. Dress in conservative clothes.
2. Instruct the attorney to ask specific questions to trigger your memory.
3. Prepare adequately. Don't memorize the testimony. Be spontaneous; such responses are more believable. Use visual aids where appropriate.
4. Prepare for testimony by acquainting yourself with the following:
   a. Be knowledgeable of five or six studies that are current and that address diagnostic issues.
   b. Know with accuracy the social, work, family, and health history of the client.
   c. Make detailed records of all contacts with client and attorneys.
   d. Review clearly all diagnostic data and be clear on your interpretation of all testing materials.
5. Do not bring a case record of the medical history into the courtroom but know what is in the record. Many times there are inconsistencies in your personal record and a good attorney will try to use this against you.

BEHAVIOR IN THE COURTROOM

1. It is important to be clear, specific, precise and articulate. Do not use empty adjectives, direct quotations, words that dramatize. Do not be repetitious.
2. Be sincere and dignified, but warm. Make eye contact with the judge and jury.
3. Never use slang or psychological jargon. When technical terms are used, define each word clearly and simply for the court.

4. Answer questions that are asked; if you don't know, don't guess, say you don't know. Saying you don't know makes you more believable.
5. Allow the attorney to develop your testimony.
6. Be aware of how you handle your anxiety. For example, some individuals slouch down when they are anxious, or speak too loud or too soft. These behaviors make the witness less credible.

SPECIFIC ISSUES IN CROSS-EXAMINATION

Often an attorney will present you with what he or she describes as new information in an effort to get you to contradict yourself and thereby weaken your testimony. Be aware that this is a strategy used by the attorney. How you respond is critical if the court is going to find your testimony believable. The following are examples of specific cross-examination:

1. The hypothetical question: "Would your opinion be different if you knew that . . ." Be relaxed and believe that if your evaluation was valid before, it is valid now. Either respond to surprise information as hypothetical, say you don't know, or go back to your evaluation.
2. Another example: If an attorney asks, "If she read some book on how to show symptoms of acute stress disorder and knew what symptoms to report, etc.," you should respond in a relaxed, matter-of-fact manner, remember you have evaluated whether the patient was faking, stand by what you've done, then state, "It is my opinion that she . . ."
3. Attorneys often try to get you to testify on information outside your evaluation; for example, to testify regarding other people's testimony, other theories, books, articles. Always stick to your own evaluation.
4. Sometimes attorneys attack you personally or attack your entire profession. This is an indication that they are desperate.

Cross-examination is critically important. Ziskin suggests six key areas that apply to the credibility of psychology. These include the following:

a. Psychology is an inexact science and lacks a systematic theoretical framework, resulting in frequent disagreements among practitioners.
b. Diagnoses in the mental health field, including those made by psychologists and psychiatrists, are very problematic, subject to low reliability, and interrater reliability.
c. Most diagnostic measures can be critized for *reliability* and *validity* issues.
d. Clinical interviews are subject to several problems and may be influenced by the bias and prejudice of the evaluator.
e. There are specific errors, omissions, short-cuts, and biases in the evaluation and testimony of the expert.
f. The credentials of the mental health professionals are inadequate or not appropriate to the case in question.

EXPERT WITNESS QUALIFICATION STATEMENT

The following components should be addressed, summarized, and clearly understood for the health care professional who is an expert witness. Each of the factors should be known to both the attorney and to the witness.

1. Name
2. Occupation/profession
3. Present practice of profession
4. Length of time in profession
5. Location of office
6. License to practice
7. Date of license
8. Professional degrees
9. Dates and schools where degrees have been obtained
10. Additional training
11. Dates of training
12. Nature, duration, and place of training
13. Professional associations
14. Articles published

15. Teaching/training experience
16. Number of investigations/evaluations
17. Number of cases (families and children) in practice
18. Previous qualification as expert witness
19. Date and court where you appeared as an expert witness

SOURCES OF STRESS IN THE COURTROOM FOR CHILD OR ADULT WITNESS

- Revealing sexually intimate details;
- The overall courtroom atmosphere;
- Repeated interrogations;
- Cross-examination by the perpetrator's attorney;
- Having to face the perpetrator, who is often a known and trusted adult;
- Guilt and fear of abusing parent going to jail;
- Family conflict, pressures, and humiliation;
- Guilt and fear of the family breaking up.

In addition, the psychological effects which result from the stresses associated with the legal system can be substantial and may include a sense of hopelessness, a sense of insignificance, feelings, guilt, fear, distrust, embarrassment, and humiliation.

Society, through its system of administering justice, requires that a person charged with an offense has a right to trial, to be confronted and to be cross-examined by those who have brought the charge.

1. Providing psychological support;
2. Interpreting the routine courtroom protocol;
3. Neutralizing the stressful feelings that may develop between the victim and people encountered in the court process.

Factors that increase stress have been identified as including the following:

1. The public setting of the courtroom and presence of the media.

2. Being unfamiliar with a courtroom and court personnel.
3. Being sequestered and seeing no familiar faces in the court.
4. Confusing questions under cross-examination and/or the use of legal or technical jargon by the attorneys.
5. Seeing the defendant.
6. Long delays and postponements.

Factors which decrease stress include:

1. Family and/or familiar persons present throughout the preparation process.
2. Providing an overview of the court process.
3. Attorneys using language that is clear and simple.
4. Refreshing the victim's memory of the evaluation.
5. Allowing child to testify in judges' chambers via closed circuit T.V.
6. Use of shield between child witness and offender.

Appendix E

Prevention and Intervention Strategies for Victims of Abuse

- Be aware of who else is around you.
- Wait a few minutes in order to be with others. If you have a choice, don't walk alone.
- Stay on populated, well-lighted streets.
- If possible, avoid dark or concealed areas—consider open areas—walk in the street if it appears to be safer.
- If you think someone is following you:
  ——Turn around and check so you're not caught off guard.
  ——Cross the street, change direction.
  ——Walk or run toward people, traffic.
  ——Consider confronting the person.
  ——Do anything necessary to enter an occupied building.
- If a car follows you or stops, do not approach the car. Change directions, walk or run toward other people, stores, or a house.

- Park in well-lighted areas at night. Check the street before leaving the car.
- Walk to your car with key ready.
- Check the backseat before you get into your vehicle.
- While driving, keep doors locked at all times.
- Keep enough gas in your tank for emergencies.
- If you're followed by another car, drive to a police or fire station, or hospital emergency entrance or any open business or gas station.
- If your car breaks down, lift hood, put on flashers.

Appendix F

National Resource Network for Child and Family Mental Health Service Sites

San Mateo County Mental Health
225 West 37th Avenue
San Mateo, CA 94403

Riverside County Mental Health/Child's Services
P.O. Box 7549
Riverside, CA 92513-7549

Solano County Mental Health Child and Adolescent Services
1735 Enterprise Drive, Bldg #3
Fairfield, CA 94533

Ventura County Mental Health Child and Adolescent Services
300 Hillmont Avenue
Ventura, CA 93003-1699

Santa Cruz County Children's Mental Health
2901 Park Avenue, D-1
Soquel, CA 95073

Sonoma County Department of Health Services
3333 Chanate Road
Santa Rose, CA 95404

Santa Barbara County Department of Mental Health Services
300 N San Antonio Road
Santa Barbara, CA 93110

Leeward Oahu Children's Team
94299 Farrington Highway
Waipahu, HI 96797

Waianae Children's Team
85-670 Farrington Highway
Waianne, HI 96792

LADSE
1301 West Cossit Avenue
LaGrange, IL 60525

Labette Center for Mental Health Services
P.O. Box 258
Parson, Kansas 67357

Sedgwick County Department of Mental Health
7701 East Kellogg
Suite 300
Wichita, KS 67207

Elizabeth Levinson Center
159 Hogan Road
Bangor, ME 04401

East Baltimore Mental Health Partnership
1235 Monument Street
Baltimore, MD 21205

Program Director
P.O. Box 668
Las Cruces, NM 88004

Alchini Binitsekees Naholzhooh Foundation, Inc.
P.O. Box 164
Tohatchi, NM 87325

New York State Office of Mental Health
New York City Regional Office
275 7th Avenue, 16th Floor
New York, NY 10001-6708

Edgecombe-Nash County Area MH/DD/SAS Authority
500 Nash Medical Arts Hall
Rocky Mount, NC 27804

Pitt Mental Health Center
203 Government Circle
Greenville, NC 27834

Department of Human Services
600 East Boulevard Avenue
Bismark, ND 58505-0271

Stark County Community Mental Health Board
800 Market Avenue North
Canton, OH 44702-1075

Southern Consortium for Children
P.O. Box 956
Athens, OH 45701-0956

Department of Health and Human Services of Lane County
125 East 8th Avenue
Eugene, OR 97401

Philadelphia Department of Public Health
1600 Arch Street, 7th Floor
Philadelphia, PA 19103

Rhode Island Department of Children, Youth and Families
610 Mt. Pleasant Avenue
Building #2
Providence, RI 02908

Charleston/Dorchester Community Mental Health
3346 Rivers Avenue
Suite D-1
N. Charleston, SC 29405

Department of Mental Health and Mental Retardation
103 South Maine
Waterbury, VT 05671-1601

Alexandria Community Services Board
720 N. Saint Asaph Street
4th Floor
Alexandria, VA 22314-1960

Milwaukee County Mental Health Complex
9501 Watertown Plank Road
Milwaukee, WI 53226

Appendix G

Confidentiality Exceptions

It is the policy of the ___________(name)___________ Counseling Center to keep confidential what is told privately in therapy sessions. There are five exceptions to this policy:

1. Mandatory reporting of child/adult abuse—KRS 620.030 states that "any person who knows or has reasonable cause to believe that a child is dependent, neglected or abused" must report the same. KRS 209 mandates the same for reporting adult abuse, which includes spouse abuse.
2. Duty to warn obligation____(state statute)____ mandates all mental health professionals to warn intended victims of client's threats of violence. Any threats of violence must be reported to any identified person and proper law enforcement authorities. In the absence of an identified person, law enforcement authorities alone are contacted.
3. When a therapist judges a client to be at immediate risk for suicide and/or in need of emergency hospitalization, confidentiality is waived for the protection of the client.

Adapted with permission from Jessamine Counseling Center, Jessamine County, Kentucky.

4. Clients who are court ordered to attend therapy are requested to sign a release of information as often the referring court wishes to monitor attendance in therapy.
5. In civil suits, where the client places his/her mental health as an issue in the suit, confidentiality is waived by the client.

References

Abramowicz, M., Ed. (1989), Ovral as a "morning-after" contraceptive. *The Medical Letter*, 31(803):93–94

ABC NEWS (1995), *ABC News 20/20 Transcript #1524*. ABC NEWS.

Albrecht, G., Walker, V., & Levy, J. (1982), Social distance from the stigmatized: A test of two theories. *Soc. Sci. & Med.*, 16:1319–1327.

American Academy of Child and Adolescent Psychiatry (1990), Guidelines for the clinical evaluation of child and adolescent sexual abuse. *Journal of Child and Adolescent Psychiatry,* 33:313–319.

American Academy of Pediatrics, Committee on Adolescence (1995), Sexual assault and the adolescent. *Pediatrics,* 94:761–765.

American Medical Association, Council on Scientific Affairs (1987), Elder abuse and neglect. *J. Amer. Med. Assn.*, 257:966.

——— Council on Ethical and Judicial Affairs (1991), Sexual misconduct in the practice of medicine. *J. Amer. Med. Assn.*, 266(8):1087–1096.

——— Council on Scientific Affairs (1993), Adolescents as victims of family violence. *J. Amer. Med. Assn.*, 257:966.

——— (1994), *Report on Violence against Women: Relevance for Medical Practitioners.* Chicago, IL: A.M.A.

American Psychiatric Association (1985), *Principles of Medical Ethics and Annotations Especially Applicable to Psychiatry.* Washington, DC: American Psychiatric Press.

——— (1987), *Diagnostic and Statistical Manual of Mental Disorders,* 3rd ed. rev. (DSM-III-R). Washington, DC: American Psychiatric Press.

——— (1994a), *Diagnostic and Statistical Manual of Mental Disorders,* 4th ed. (DSM-IV). Washington, DC: American Psychiatric Press.

——— (1994b), *Fact Sheet on Memories of Sexual Abuse.* Washington, DC: American Psychiatric Press.

American Psychoanalytic Association (1993), *Principles of Ethics for Psychoanalysis and Provisions for Implementation of the Principles of Ethics for Psychoanalysis.* New York: American Psychoanalytic Association.

American Psychological Association (1980), *Ethical Principles of Psychologists.* Washington, DC: American Psychological Association.

——— (1995a), *Task Force Report on Domestic Violence.* Washington, DC: American Psychological Association.

——— (1995b), Working group on investigation of memories of childhood abuse. *National Center for Prosecution of Child Abuse,* 8:36–42. Washington, DC: American Psychological Association.

Americans with Disabilities Act (1990), (P.L. 101–336, approved July 26, 1990).

Asher, S. R., & Coie, J. D., Eds. (1990), *Peer Rejection in Childhood.* Cambridge, MA: Cambridge University Press.

Bagley, C. (1989), *Utility of the Trauma Symptom Checklist in Screening For Young Women Who Experience Serious Sexual Abuse in Childhood.* Typescript.

Bass, E., & Davis, E. (1988), *The Course to Heal.* New York: Harper & Row.

Beane, A. (1996), *Handbook to Promote the Acceptance of Employees with Disabilities.* Unpublished manuscript.

Becker, J. V., Kaplan, M. S., Tenke, C. E., & Tartaglini, P. N. (1991), The incidence of depressive symptomatology in juvenile sex offenders with a history of abuse. *Child Abuse & Neglect,* 15(3):531–536.

Biden, J. R., Jr. (1993), Violence against women: The congressional response. *Amer. Psychologist,* 48(5):1058–1060.

Blake, W., Wethers, P., Nagy, R., & Friedman, M. (1993), *Clinician-Administered PTSD Scale (CAPS).* Boston: National Center for PTSD, Behavioral Sciences Division.

Blanchard, E. B. (1990), Biofeedback treatment of essential hypertension. *Biofeedback & Self-Regu.,* 15(9):209–228.

Blume, E. (1990). *Secret Survivors: Uncovering Incest and its After Effects in Women.* New York: John Wiley.

Boehnlein, J. K., & Kinzie, J. D. (1995), Cross-cultural assessment of traumatization. In: *Theory and Assessment of Stressful Life Events,* ed. T. W. Miller. Madison, CT: International Universities Press.

——— ——— Fleck, J. (1992), DSM diagnosis of posttraumatic stress disorder and cultural sensitivity: A response. *Nerv. & Ment.*, 180(6):597–599.

——— Sparr, L. F. (1993), Group therapy for WWII ex-POW's: Long-term posttraumatic adjustment in a geriatric population. *Amer. J. Psychother.*, 47(4):273–282.

Bordieri, J., & Drehmer, D. (June, 1987), Attribution of responsibility and predicted social acceptance of disabled workers. *Rehab. Counsel. Bull.*, 30(4):218–226.

Bowlby, J. G. (1969), *Attachment and Loss.* New York: Basic Books.

Brady v. Hopper, 570 F.Suppl. 1333 (D. Colo. 1983).

Braver, J. G., Blumberg, J., Green, K., & Rawson, R. (1992), Childhood abuse and current psychological functioning in a university counseling center population. *Counsel Psychol.*, 39(3):252–257.

Briere, J. (1984), The effects of childhood sexual abuse on later psychological functioning: Defining a post-sexual abuse syndrome. Paper presented at the Third National Conference on Sexual Victimization of Children, Children's Hospital National Medical Center, Washington, DC.

——— (1992), *Child Abuse Trauma: Theory and Treatment of Lasting Effects.* Newbery Park, CA: Sage.

——— Runtz, M. (1989). The Trauma Symptom Checklist. Early data on a new scale. *Interpers. Viol.*, 4(3):151–163.

——— ——— (1992), The Trauma Symptom Inventory, *Child Abuse & Neglect,* 12(5):331–341.

Brodsky, A. M. (1989), Sex between patient and therapist: Psychology's data and response. In: *Sexual Exploitation in Professional Relationships,* ed. G. Gabbard. Washington, DC: American Psychiatric Press, pp. 15–25.

Browne, A. (1991), The victim's experience: Pathways to disclosure. *Psychother.*, 28(3):150–156.

——— (1992), Violence against women: Relevance for medical practitioners (Report on the Council on Scientific Affairs, American Medical Association). *J. Amer. Med. Assn.*, 267(23):3184–3189.

——— Finkelhor, D. (1986), Impact of child sexual abuse: A review of the research. *Psychol. Bull.*, 99(1):66–77.

Burge, E. B. (1982), Child abusive attitudes and life changes in an overseas military environment. *Diss. Abstra. Internat.*, 43, 562A.

Burgess, A., & Hartman, C. R. (1993), *Sexual Exploitation of Patients by Health Professionals.* New York: Praeger.

——— Hazelwood, R. R., Rokous, F. E., & Hartman, C. R. (1993), Serial rapists and their victims: Reenactment and repetition. *Annals Acad. Sci.*, 528:277–295.

——— Holstrom, V. (1979), Rape trauma syndrome. Address, Annual Meeting of the American Psychiatric Association, Washington, DC.

Burgess, R. L. (1979), Child Abuse: A social interactional analysis. In: *Advances in Clinical Child Psychology,* ed. B. B. Lahey & A. E. Kazdin. New York: Plenum Press, pp. 1410–172.

Byrne, B. (1993), *Coping with Bullying in Schools.* Dublin: The Columbia Press.

——— (1994), *Bullying: A Community Approach.* Mount Merrion, Blackrock, Co Dublin: The Columbia Press.

Campbell, J. (1994), Domestic homicide: risk assessment and professional duty to warn. *MD Med. J.,* 43:885–889.

Cantrell, B., Harmon, K., Alarte, C., Philstein, F., & Lacalio, C. (1989), Psychiatrist–patient sexual contact: Results of a national survey. 1, Prevalence, *Amer. J. Psychiatry,* 143:1126–1131.

Centers for Disease Control (1991), *Healthy People 2000: National Health Promotion and Disease Prevention Objectives.* Washington, DC: USDHHS.

Centers for Disease Control (1993a), Sexually transmitted diseases—Treatment guidelines. *MMWR,* 42:1–102.

——— (1993b), CDC alert. Preventing homicide in the workplace. Washington, DC: USDHHS (NIOSH) publication No. 93–109.

Cicchetti, D., & Olsen, K. (1987), The develolpmental psychopathology of child maltreatment. In: *Handbook of Developmental Psychopathology,* ed. M. Lewis and S. Miller. New York: Plenum Press.

Clark, B., & Miller, T. W. (1996), Clinical models of traumatization in children. In: *Children of Trauma,* ed. T. W. Miller. Madison, CT: International Universities Press.

Conte, J. R., Berliner, L., & Schuerman, J. R. (1987), *The Impact of Sexual Abuse on Children.* Finial Technical Report. Rockville, MD: National Institute of Mental Health, Project Number MH 37133.

Dadds, M., Smith, M., & Webber, Y. (1991), An exploration of family and individual profiles following father–daughter incest. *Child Abuse & Neglect,* 15(2):575–586.

Davidson, J. T., & Foa, E. B. (1991), Diagnostic issues in posttraumatic stress disorder: Considerations for the DSM-IV. *Abnorm. Psychology,* 100(4):346–355.

DeJong, A. R. (1985), The medical evaluation of sexual abuse in children. *Hosp. Commun. Psychiatry,* 36(3):405–509.

Derman, B., with Hauge, M. (1994), *We'd Have a Great Relationship If It Weren't For You.* Deerfield Beach, FL: Health Communications.

Dershowitz, A. (1995). *The Abuse Excuse.* Boston: Little Brown. Publishers.

DiVasto, P., Kaufman, A., & Jackson, R. (1980), Caring for rape victims: Its impact on providers. *J. Comm. Health,* 5:204–208.

Dohrenwend, B. S., Raphael, K., Schwartz, S., Stueve, A., & Skodol, A. (1993), Structured event probe and narrative rating method for measuring stressful life events. In: *Handbook of Stress* (2nd ed.), ed. L. Goldberger & S. Breznitz. New York: Free Press.

Duluth Abuse Intervention Project, Municipal Government of Duluth, Minnesota (1992), *Preliminary Report on Domestic Violence.*

Dutton, K., & Painter, L. (1981), *Traumatic Bonding Theory, Issues and Considerations.* Unpublished.

Dwyer, J., Stewart, G., & McDonald, P. (1993), The rational use of the HIV antibody test. *Med. J. Australia,* 158:327–328.

Edelson, J. L. (1985), Group treatment for men who batter. *Soc. Work Res. & Abstr.,* 86(4):264–272.

Elliot, D. M. (1990), *The Effects of Childhood Sexual Abuse on Adult Functioning on a National Sample of Professional Women.* Unpublished doctoral dissertation, Biola University, Rose Mead School of Professional Psychology, Los Angeles, CA.

——— Briere, J. M. (1992), Sexual abuse trauma: Validating the Trauma Symptom Checklist (TSC-40). *Child Abuse & Neglect,* 16:391–398.

Fagan, J., & Browne, A. (1993), Violence between spouses and intimates: Physical aggression between women and in intimate relationships. In: *Understanding and Preventing Violence,* Vol. 3, ed. A. Reiss, Jr. & J. Roth. Washington, DC: National Academy Press.

Farber, E., Kinast, C., McCoard, W. (1984), Violence in Families of Adolescent Runaways. *Child Abuse & Negl.,* 8:295–299.

Ferenczy, A. (1995), Epidemiology and clinical pathophysiology of condyloma accuminata. *Amer. J. Obstet. Gynecol.,* 172:1331–1339.

Figley, C. R. (1984), *Sexually Victimized Children.* New York: Free Press.

——— Ed. (1985), *Trauma and Its Wake: The Study and Treatment of Post-Traumatic Stress Disorder.* New York: Brunner/Mazel.

Finkelhor, D. (1984), *Sexually Victimized Children.* New York: Free Press.

Flitcraft, A. (1992), *Diagnostic and Treatment Guidelines on Domestic Violence.* Chicago, IL: American Medical Association.

Florian, V. (1978), Employer's opinions of the disabled person as a worker. *Rehab. Counsel. Bull.,* 22:38–43.

Floyd, N. M. (1987), Terrorism in the schools. *School Safety,* Winter: 22–25.

Foa, E. B., Riggs, D., Dancer, C. V., & Rothbaum, O. (1993), Reliability and validity of a brief instrument for assessing post-traumatic stress disorder. *J. Trauma & Stress,* 6(4):459–473.

Freyd, J. (1996), *Betrayal Trauma: The Logic of Forgetting Childhood Abuse.* Cambridge, MA: Harvard University Press.

Friedman, M. (1991), Neurological alteration association with posttraumatic stress disorder. National Center for PTSD, Clinical Laboratory and Education Division, Teleconference Report, July.

——— (1993), Neurological alterations associated with post-traumatic stress disorder. National Center for PTSD, Clinical Laboratory and Education Division, Teleconference Report, July.

Gabbard, G. O. (1991), Psychodynamics of sexual boundary violations. *Psychiatric Annals.,* 211:651–655.

Garbarino, J., Guttman, E., & Seeley, J. (1986), *The Psychologically Battered Child: Strategies for Identification, Assessment and Intervention.* San Francisco: Jossey-Bass.

Gartrell, G., Herman, J., Olante, S., Feldstein, H., & Localio, S. (1987), Reported practices of psychiatrists who knew of sexual misconduct by colleagues. *Amer. J. Orthopsychiatry,* 57(2):287–289.

Gelles, R. (1987), *Family Violence.* Beverly Hills, CA: Sage.

Gin, N., Rucker, L., Frayne, S., & Hibbard, R. A. (1991), Prevalence of domestic violence among patients of three ambulatory care internal medicine clinics. *J. Gen. Intern. Med.,* 6:317–322.

Gise, L., & Paddison, P. (1988), Rape, sexual abuse and its victims. *Psychiat. Clin. N. Amer.,* 11(4):629–648.

Goffman, E. (1963), *Stigma.* Englewood Cliffs, NJ: Prentice Hall.

Gold, E. (1986), Long-term effects of sexual victimization in childhood: An attributional approach. *Consult. & Clin. Psychol.,* 54(4):471–475.

Goldberg, W., & Tomlanovich, M. (1984), Domestic violence in the emergency department. *J. Amer. Med. Assn.,* 34(6):251–259.

Goldberger, L., & Breznitz, S., Eds. (1993), *Handbook of Stress,* 2nd. ed. New York: Free Press.

Gomez-Schwartz, B., Horowitz, J. M., & Sauzier, M. (1985), Severity of emotional distress among sexually abused preschool, school-age, and adolescent children. *Hosp. & Commun. Psychiatry,* 36(3):503–508.

Goodyear, I. M. (1990), Family relationships, life events and childhood psychopathology. *Child Psychiatry & Psychol. Allied Disciplines,* 31(1):161–192.

Green, B. (1990), Defining trauma: Terminology and generic stress dimensions. *J. Appl. Soc. Psychol.,* 20(11):1632–1642.

——— Wilson, J., & Lindy, J. (1985), Conceptualizing post-traumatic stress disorder: A psychosocial framework. In: *Trauma and Its Wake,* ed. C. Figley. New York: Brunner/Mazel, pp. 386–389.

Hall, D. (1995), *Jump Start Your Brain.* New York: Warner Books.

Hammerberg, J. (1992), *The PEN Inventory.* Typescript.

Hart, S. N., & Brassard, M. R. (1987), A major threat to children's mental health: Psychological maltreatment. *Amer. Psychologist,* 42(2): 160–165.

Harvard Mental Health Letter (1993), Clinical issues in abuse & neglect. (11):31–32.

Heap, K. K. (1991), A predictive and follow up study of abusive and neglectful families by case analysis. *Child Abuse & Neglect,* 15(1):261–273.

Hedlund v. Superior Court of Orange City (1983), 669 P.2d 41, 191 Cal. Rptr. 805.

Helton, A., McFarlane, J., & Anderson, E. (1987), Battered and pregnant: A prevalence study. *Amer. J. Public Health,* 77:1337–1339.

Herman, J. L. (1981), *Father–Daughter Incest.* Cambridge, MA: Harvard University Press.

——— (1992), *Trauma and Recovery.* New York: Basic Books.

Hibbard, R. A., & Zollinger, G. W. (1990), Patterns of child sexual abuse knowledge amongst professionals. *Child Abuse & Neglect,* 14(5): 347–495.

Holtz, H., Esposito, C., & Podhorin, R. (1994), Part 1: A domestic violence primer for clinicians. *New Eng. J. Med.,* 91:848–850.

——— ——— ——— (1994), Part 2: A domestic violence primer for clinicians. *New Eng. J. Med.,* 91:853–854.

Horowitz, M. J. (1986), Stress response syndromes: A review of post traumatic and adjustment disorders. *Hosp. & Commun. Psychiatry,* 37(2):241–249.

——— Field, N. P., & Classen, C. C. (1993), Stress response syndromes and their treatment. In: *Handbook of Stress,* 2nd ed., ed. L. Goldberger & S. Breznitz. New York: Free Press, pp. 757–774.

——— Wilner, N., & Alvarez, W. (1979), Impact of Event Scale: A measure of subjective stress. *Psychosom. Med.,* 41(2):209–218.

Human Abuse Prevention Council (1994), *Annual Report on Epidemiological Factors of Human Abuse.* Duluth, MI: Municipal Government Center.

Jablonski by Pahls v. U.S., 712 F.2d 391 (9th Cir. 1983).

Jackson, H., & Muttal, R. (1993), Clinical responses to sexual abuse allegations. *Child Abuse & Neglect,* 17(6):127–143.

Jacobson, A., Koehler, J., & Jones-Brown, C. (1987), The failure of routine assessment to detect histories of assault experiences by psychiatric patients. *Hosp. & Commun. Psychiatry,* 38(5):386–389.

Jacobson, N. (1995), Clinical Significance of Adjustment in Abuse. Cape Cod Seminars, Cape Cod, Mass. (Seminar Presentation)

Johnson, M. K., Hashprode, S., & Lindsay, D. S. (1993), Source monitoring. *Psychol. Bull.,* 114:3–28.

Joiner, L., Beane, A., & Grant, P. (1975), After desegregation: Suggestions for promoting social integration of handicapped children in regular classes. Paper presented at the Annual Illinois Council for Exceptional Children Convention, Chicago.

Joint Commission on Accreditation of Healthcare Organizations (1992), *Accreditation Manual for Hospitals.* Oakbrook Terrace, IL: Author.

Jones, J., & Fay, L. (1988), The Childcare Attitude Inventory. *Psycholog. Rep.,* 63(3):841–842.

Jordan, C., & Walker, R. (1995), Responding to complaints of sexual misconduct by licensed and certified professionals. In: *Guidelines for Licensure Boards.* Frankfort, KY: Kentucky Board of Occupations and Professions.

Jorgenson, L. M. (1994), Sexual boundary violations. *Treatment Today,* 6(2):224–238.

Kapp, M. B. (1995), Elder mistreatment: Legal interventions and policy uncertainties. *Behav. Sci. & the Law,* 13:365–380.

Katz, I. (1981), *Stigma: A Social Psychological Analysis.* Hillsdale, NJ: Lawrence Erlbaum.

Katz, R. C. (1990), Psychosocial adjustment in adolescent child molesters. *Child Abuse & Neglect,* 14(1):567–575.

Keane, T. M., Caddell, J. M., & Taylor, K. L. (1988), The Mississippi Scale for Combat-Related PTSD: Three studies in reliability and validity. *Consult. & Clin. Psychol.,* 56(2):85–90.

Kenney, J. (1993), *Preventing Workplace Violence.* Chicago, IL: National Safe Workplace Institute.

Kentucky Society of Clinical Social Work (1996), *Safety in Therapy: Guidelines for Clinicians.* Lexington, KY: Kentucky Society of Clinical Social Work.

Kidder, L. H., & Stewart, M. V. (1975), *The Psychology of Intergroup Relations: Conflict and Consciousness.* New York: McGraw-Hill.

Kilbury, R., Bordieri, J., & Wong, H. (1996), Impact of physical disability and gender on personal space. *J. Rehab.,* 62(2):59–61.

Kilpatrick, D. (1987), Incident report interview. Transcript for the *Diagnostic and Statistical Manual.* Washington, DC: American Psychiatric Association.

——— Resnick, H. S., Saunders, B. E., & Best, C. L. (1989), *The National Women's Study PTSD Module.* Charleston, SC: Crime Victims Research and Treatment Center, Department of Psychiatry, Medical University of South Carolina. Unpublished instrument.

——— ——— Freedy, J. R. (1991), *The Potential Stressful Events Interview.* Charleston, SC: Crime Victims Research and Treatment Center, Department of Psychiatry, Medical University of South Carolina. Unpublished instrument.

Kluft, R. P. (1990), *Incest-Related Syndromes of Adult Psychopathology.* Washington, DC: American Psychiatric Press.

Korbin, J. E. (1989), Fatal maltreatment by mothers: A proposed framework. *Child Abuse & Neglect,* 13(3):481–489.

Krugman, S. (1987), Trauma in the family: Perspectives on the intergenerational transmission of violence. In: *Psychological trauma,* ed. B. A. van der Kolk. Washington, DC: American Psychiatric Press, pp. 127–152.

Kulka, R. A., Schlenger, W. E., Fairbank, J. A., Hough, R. L., Jordan, B. K., Marmar, C. R., & Weiss, D. S. (1990), *Contractual Report of Findings from the National Vietnam Veterans Readjustment Society.* Research Triangle Park, NC: Research Triangle Institute.

Lachs, L., & Fulmer, T. (1993), Recognizing elder abuse and neglect. *Clin. Geriatr. Med.,* 9:665–675.

Lindsay, K., & Reed, J. (1995), Clinical issues and false memory syndrome. In: American Psychological Association Task Force on Domestic Violence. Washington, DC: American Psychological Association, pp. 148–156.

Loftus, E. (1993), *The Reality of Repressed Memories.* Washington, DC: American Psychological Association Task Force on Repressed Memory.

——— Coan, D. (1995), The construction of childhood memories. In: *The Child Witness in Context: Cognitive, Social and Legal Perspectives,* ed. D. P. Peters. New York: Kauwr Press.

Loring, M., & Smith, R. (1994), Health care barriers and interventions for battered women. *Pub. Health Rep.,* 109:328–338.

MacIan, P. S., & Perlman, P. A. (1992), Development and Use of the TST Life Event Questionnaire. *Treating Abuse Today,* 2(1):9–11.

McCann, I. L., & Pearlman, L. A. (1990), *Psychological Trauma and the Adult Survivor: Theory, Therapy, and Transformation.* New York: Brunner/Mazel.

——— Sakheim, D. K., & Abrahamson, D. J. (1988), Trauma and victimization: A model of psychological adaptation. *Counsel. Psychologist,* 16(4):531–594.

McFarlane, J., Parker, B., Soeken, K. (1992), Assessing for abuse during pregnancy. *J.A.M.A.,* 267:3176–3178.

McFarland, K. (1992), Assessing for abuse during pregnancy. *J. Amer. Med. Assn.,* 267(8):3176–3183.

——— Waterman, J. (1988), *Domestic Abuse.* New York: Guilford Press.

Medgyesi, V. (1996), The chrome ceiling: When just having a job isn't enough. *New Mobility,* 7(37):26–30.

Megana, D. (1990), *The Impact of Client–Therapist Sexual Intimacy and Child Sexual Abuse on Psychosocial and Psychological Functioning.* Unpublished doctoral dissertation, University of California, Los Angeles, CA.

Miller, T. W. (1993), The assessment of stressful life events. *Internat. J. Soc. Psychiatry,* 25(2):320–325.

——— Kraus, R. F. (1995), Theoretical models of stress adaptation. In: *Theory and Assessment of Stressful Life Events,* ed. T. W. Miller. Madison, CT: International Universities Press, pp. 93–107.

——— ——— Kamenchko, P., & Krasnianski, A. (1993), Post traumatic stress disorder in U.S. and Russian veterans. *Hosp. & Commun. Psychiatry,* 44(3):585–587.

——— Miller, J. M., & Veltkamp, L. J. (1993), Dimensions of family violence: Recognition and referral. *Amer. J. Occupa. Ther.,* 18(3):28–34.

——— Veltkamp, L. J. (1986), Use of fables in clinical assessment of contested-child custody. *Child Psychiatry & Hum. Develop.,* 16(4):272–284.

——— ——— (1988), Effects of multi-generational sexual abuse in rural America. *Internat. J. Fam. Psychiatry,* 9(3):257–275.

——— ——— (1989a), The abusing family in rural America. *Internat. J. Fam. Psychiatry,* 9(3):259–275.

——— ——— (1989b), Effect of child sexual abuse: The adult non-survivor. *J. KY Med. Assn.,* 87(1):120–124.

——— ——— (1993), Family violence: Clinical indicators among military and post-military personnel. *Milit. Med.,* 158(12):766–771.

Milner, J. S. (1980), *Child Abuse Potential Inventory.* Typescript.

Mollica, R. F., Wyshak, G., Lavelle, J., Truong, R., Tor, S., & Yang, T. (1990), Assessing symptom change in Southeast Asian refugee survivors of mass violence and torture. *Amer. J. Psychiatry,* 147(2):83–88.

Monahan, J. (1981), *The Clinical Prediction of Violent Behavior.* Washington, DC: U.S. Government Printing Office.

Morris, J. (1994), It's ok to be an introvert. *Edu. Digest,* 60(4):61–62.

National Center on Child Abuse and Neglect (1988), *Executive Summary: National Study of the Incidence and Severity of Child Abuse and Neglect.* Washington, DC: U.S. Government Printing Office.

Ney, P. G. (1988), Triangle of abuse: A model of maltreatment. *Child Abuse & Neglect,* 12(2):363–373.

Nichols, A. R., & Molinder, I. (1984), Multi-phasic Sexual Inventory. Typescript.

Norris, F. H. (1990), Screening for traumatic stress: A scale for use in the general population. *J. Applied Soc. Psychol.,* 20:1704–1718.

O'Brien, M., & Bera, W. (1986), Adolescent sexual offenders: A descriptive topology. *Preventing Sexual Abuse,* 1(3):3–5.

Oden, S. (1981), A child's social isolation: Origins, prevention, intervention. In: *Teaching Social Skills to Children,* ed. G. Catledge & J. F. Milburn. New York: Pergamon Press.

Olante, S. W. (1991), Characteristics of therapist who become involved in sexual boundary violations. *Psychiatric Annals,* 21:657–660.

O'Rourke, W. (1981), Seven theories related to elder abuse. Grand rounds presentation. Department of Psychiatry, University of Michigan, Ann Arbor, Michigan. April 15.

Paymer, M. (1996), *Violent No More.* Alexander, CA: Hunter House.

Pfenninger, J. (1989), Androscopy: A technique for examining men for condyloma. *J. Fam. Pract.,* 29:286–288.

Pitman, R. K. (1988), Post-traumatic stress disorder, conditioning, and network therapy. *Psychiatric Annals,* 18:181–189.

Pollick, M. (1987), Abuse of the elderly: A review. *Holistic Nursing Practice,* 12(2):47–53.

Pontius, A. A. (1988), Introduction to biological issues, with neuropathological case illustrations. *Annals N.Y. Acad. Sci.,* 52(8):148–153.

Pope, K. K. (1986), Research and laws regarding therapist–patient sexual involvement: Implications for therapists. *Amer. J. Psychother.,* 40(6):564.

Popma, J. (1995), *The Impact of Psychologist's Knowledge, Attitudes, and Training on Survivors of Childhood Sexual Abuse.* Unpublished doctoral dissertation, University of Kentucky, Lexington, Kentucky.

Putnam, F. W. (1989), *Diagnosis and Treatment of Multiple Personality Disorder.* New York: Guilford Press.

Pynoos, R. S., & Nadar, K. (1989), Children's memory and proximity to violence. *J. Amer. Acad. Child & Adol. Psychiatry,* 36(5):236–241.

Remer, P. (1986), *Stages in Coping with Rape.* University of Kentucky. Typescript.

Resnick, H., Best, C., Kilpatrick, D., Freedy, J. R., & Falsetti, S. (1993), Assessment of civilian rated post traumatic stress disorder. In: *Theory and Assessment of Stressful Life Events,* ed. T. W. Miller. Madison, CT: International Universities Press.

Rieker, P., & Carmen, E. (1986), The victim-to-patient process: The disconfirmation and transformation of abuse. *Amer. J. Orthopsychiatry,* 56(3):360–370.

Ross, C. A., Heber, S., Norton, G. R., Anderson, D., Anderson, G., & Barchett, P. (1989), *The Dissociative Disorders Interview Schedule: A Structured Interview.* New York: John Wiley.

Sankin, D., & Durphy, M. (1982), *Learning to Live without Violence.* San Francisco: Volcano Press.

Schatzow, E., & Herman, J. L. (1989), Breaking secrecy. Adult survivors disclose to their families. *Psychiat. Clin. N. Amer.,* 12(2):337–349.

Schoener, G., Milgram, J., Gonsiorek, E., Luepker, M., & Conroe, E. (1989), Psychotherapists sexual involvement with clients. *Intervent. & Prevent.,* 34(4):137–142.

Scott, C., & Matricciani, R. (1994), Joint Commission on Accreditation of Healthcare Organizations standards to improve care for victims of abuse. *MD Med. J.,* 43:891–898.

Scurfield, R. M. (1985), Post trauma stress assessment and treatment: Overview and formulations. In: *Trauma and Its Weight: The Study and Treatment of Post Traumatic Stress Disorder,* ed. C. R. Figley. New York: Brunner/Mazel.

Select Committee on Aging (1980), *Domestic Violence Against the Elderly.* Hearings before the Subcommittee on Human Services, House of Representatives, April 21. Washington, DC: U.S. Government Printing Office.

——— (1981), *Elder Abuse: An Examination of a Hidden Problem.* Washington, DC: U.S. Government Printing Office.

Sgroi, S. (1992), *Handbook on Clinical Interventions in Child Sexual Abuse.* Boston: Lexington Books.

Shapiro, F. (1995), *Eye Movement Desensitization and Reprocessing: Basic Principles, Protocols, and Procedures.* New York: Guilford Press.

Sherif, M., Harvey, O. J., White, B. J., Hood, W. R., & Sherif, C. W. (1961), *Intergroup Conflict and Cooperation.* Norman, OK: University of Oklahoma.

Spitzer, R., Williams, E., & Gibbons, Jr. (1987), *DSM-III-R Casebook.* Washington, DC: American Psychiatric Press.

Steele, B. F. (1986), Notes on the lasting effects of early child abuse throughout the life cycle. *Child Abuse & Neglect,* 10(3):283–291.

Stone, L. B. (1980), *A Study of the Relationship Amongst Anxious Attachment, Ego Functioning and Female Patients' Vulnerabilities to Sexual Involvement with their Male Psychotherapists.* Los Angeles, CA, California School of Professional Psychology. Doctoral dissertation, 42:789B.

Straus, M. A., & Gelles, R. J. (1990), The national family violence survey. *Physical Violence in American families: Risk Factors and Adaption to Violence in 8,145 Families,* ed. M. A. Straus & R. J. Gelles. New Brunswick, NJ: Transaction, pp. 3–16.

Stuitz, M. (1994), The Community Public Health and Safety Act of 1994, Washington State Senate.

Sugg, N., & Innui, T. (1992), Primary care physicians' response to domestic violence: Opening Pandora's box. *J.A.M.A.,* 267:3157–3160.

Summit, R. C. (1983), The child sexual abuse accommodation syndrome. *Child Abuse & Neglect,* 7(1):177–193.

Tarasoff v. Regents of University of California, 17 Cal.3d 425, 551 P2d 334 (1976).

Thompson v. County of Alameda, 614 P.2d 728 (1980).

Taylor, C. G., Murphy, J. M., Jellink, M., Quinn, D., Poitrast, F. G., & Goshko, M. (1991). Diagnosed intellectual and emotional impairment among parents who seriously mistreat their children: Prevalence, type and outcome in a court sample. *Child Abuse & Neglect,* 15(2):389–401.

Terr, L. (1995), *Unchained Memories: True Stories and Traumatic Memories, Lost & Found.* New York: Basic Books.

Tsygankov, B., & Melanin, A. (1991), Mental disorders among Soviet veterans of the war in Afghanistan. *World Internat. Soc. Ment. Ill. & Collab.,* 3(2):18–21.

U.S. Department of Health and Human Services (1980), *Elder Abuse: Report of the Bureau of Labor Statistics to Health and Human Services.* Washington, DC: U.S. Government Printing Office.

VandeCreek, L., & Knapp, S. (1993), *Tarasoff and Beyond: Legal and Clinical Considerations in the Treatment of Life-Endangering Patients.* Sarasota, FL: Professional Resource Press.

van der Kolk, B. A. (1987), The psychological consequences of overwhelming life experiences. In: *Psychological Trauma,* ed. B. A. van der Kolk. Washington, DC: American Psychiatric Press, pp. 1–30.

——— Kadish, W. (1987), Amnesia, dissociation, and the return of the repressed. In: *Psychological Trauma,* ed. B. A. van der Kolk. Washington, DC: American Psychiatric Press, pp. 173–190.

Veltkamp, L. J., & Miller, T. W. (1994), *Clinical Handbook of Child Abuse and Neglect.* Madison, CT: International Universities Press.

——— ——— Kearl, G. W., Barlow-Elliot, L., & Bright, K. (1992), Interdisciplinary Treatment of Abused Families in Kentucky. *KY Med. Assn.,* 90:232–239.

——— ——— Silman, M. (1994), Adult non-survivors: A failure to cope with victims of child abuse. *Child Psychiatry & Hum. Develop.,* 24(4):231–243.

Vernon-Oehmke, A. (1994), *Effective Hiring and ADA Compliance.* New York: American Management Association.

Walker, L. (1979), *The Battered Woman Syndrome.* New York: Harper & Row.

——— (1992), *Terrifying Love.* New York: Plenum.

——— (1994), *Abused Women in Survivor Therapy.* Washington, DC: American Psychological Association Press.

——— (1996), *Survivor Therapy Techniques.* Hicksville, NY: Walker.

Watson, D., Clark, L. A., & Tellegen, A. (1991), Development and validation of brief measures of positive and negative affect: The PANAS Scales. *Personal & Soc. Psychol.,* 54(2):1063–1070.

Westermeyer, J. (1987), Clinical considerations in cross-cultural diagnosis. *Hosp. & Commun. Psychiatry,* 38(2):160–165.

Whipple, E. E., & Webster-Stratton, C. (1991), The role of parental stress in physical abusive families. *Child Abuse & Neglect,* 15(2):279–291.

Whittlesea, B. (1993), Illusions of trauma. *J. Experiment. Psychol.,* 19(6):1235–1253.

Williams, L. M. (1994), Recall of childhood trauma: A prospective study of women's memories of child sexual abuse. *Consult. & Clin. Psychol.,* 62(6):1167–1176.

Wohlberg, J. (1990), Psychological aspects of therapist sexual abuse. Paper presented at the Boston Psychoanalytic Society and Institute, February 10.

Worell, J., & Remer, P. (1992), *Feminist Perspectives and Therapy: An Empowerment Model for Women.* New York: John Wiley.

Wright, L., & Smye, M. (1996), *Corporate Abuse.* New York: Macmillan.

Yupze, A., & Lancee, W. (1977), Ethinyl estradiol and *dl*-norgestrel as a postcoital contraceptive. *Fertil. Steril.,* 28:932.

Zuravin, S. J. (1989), Severity of material depression and three types of mother-to-child aggression. *Amer. J. Orthopsychiatry,* 59(39): 377–389.

Name Index

Subject Index